The Elements of Pain and Conflict
in Human Life, considered from
a Christian Point of View

The Elements of Pain and Conflict in Human Life, considered from a Christian Point of View

BEING LECTURES DELIVERED AT THE
CAMBRIDGE SUMMER MEETING, 1916
BY MEMBERS OF THE UNIVERSITY

Cambridge :
at the University Press
1916

CAMBRIDGE
UNIVERSITY PRESS

University Printing House, Cambridge CB2 8BS, United Kingdom

Cambridge University Press is part of the University of Cambridge.

It furthers the University's mission by disseminating knowledge in the pursuit of
education, learning and research at the highest international levels of excellence.

www.cambridge.org
Information on this title: www.cambridge.org/9781107586154

© Cambridge University Press 1916

First published 1916
First paperback edition 2015

A catalogue record for this publication is available from the British Library

ISBN 978-1-107-58615-4 Paperback

PREFATORY NOTE

I HAVE been asked to say a few explanatory words in regard to the Course of Lectures contained in this volume. It has been customary that there should be some lectures on theological subjects at the Summer Meetings which have from time to time taken place at Cambridge in connexion with the University Local Lectures' system. The Committee of the Local Lectures, when arranging for such a Course this year, held that it ought to deal directly with those difficulties for Christian Theism which are raised by the spectacle of conflict and suffering in the world—difficulties which have long been more or less familiar to thoughtful minds, but which are, perhaps, more acutely and widely felt at the present moment, owing to the circumstances of the time, than they ever were before.

The attendance at this course of lectures, and the remarks made by many who heard them, shewed that not a few of those, who had gathered for the Summer Meeting mainly in order to hear lectures on subjects of an entirely different character, were earnestly concerned about the grave problems here treated, and grateful for any help in reflecting upon them. It is hoped that some of these hearers may be glad to have the lectures in a permanent form, and that others, too, who were not present will welcome their publication.

It should be added that there was no consultation among the lecturers as to the treatment of the subjects allotted to them, and that they are responsible only for what they have individually said. But in spite of this independence, and of the fact that the subjects of the lectures, more especially those of the first seven, are intimately connected, it will not, I think, be found that there is needless repetition, or that there are serious discrepancies of thought.

V. H. STANTON.

CAMBRIDGE,
September 21, 1916.

CONTENTS

THEISM AND MODERN THOUGHT

I

We in this age—and the same holds true for men in every age—should take stock of the old things as well as press forward in ways that are new. Our life has to face the future; but we face it with eyes that have been taught to see and hands trained to act by past experience. This past experience guides our actions almost unconsciously; so that we may think little of it or may not think of it at all. We become aware of it only when we reflect on the principles, methods and ideals of our life. In our thinking, also, we are for ever gathering new facts and shedding old ideas, and we are apt to overlook its fundamental continuity. It is the new things and not the old that attract attention; and, as our experience grows, we make our ways of organising it—our scientific methods—more swift and certain. But just because our experience is a growth, the changes in it are not mere changes—not simply the substitution of one thing for another. What is new does not entirely displace what is old; it adds to it and takes away from it; but there is always something which persists and which is modified not by disconnected jerks but by continuous stages. This continuity is a mark not only of our active life but also of our thought. In both there are permanent factors which guard the unity of the whole. And these permanent factors are always combined with other factors, which by comparison are transient; and it is not easy to disentangle them in our reflexion.

Amongst the more permanent factors in our thinking must be counted an attitude towards the world and towards life as a whole. The details of the environment demand constant attention; but the details are always changing. At first the pressing needs of living leave little room for thought; but these needs vary from day to day. Whenever men begin to reflect they go beyond the immediate details and try to form some kind of view of the nature and meaning of life as a whole. There are indeed many things which interfere with this wider view: the pressure of momentary needs; the swift change of external objects; nay, science itself—for in showing us the connexions of things in detail, it may tend to restrict our view to a narrow horizon. But the call of the whole is insistent, though it may not be loud; and so we lift our eyes from the scenery in the foreground and try to form some idea of the world as a whole and of our own place in it.

Further, in this quest there always remains an element of mystery. We cannot have a complete view of the world-whole, for its detail is infinite. And we cannot get as clear and distinct a view of it as we may have of more limited objects of knowledge. We get much more exact knowledge from the special sciences than we can ever hope to get from theology. If our thought could be hedged within the region which is sometimes called 'positive,' there would be no mystery to baffle us. But this region of 'positive' facts is itself imbedded in a wider world of experience; it cannot stand by itself, as some writers have thought. In describing it we use a set of concepts which apply very imperfectly to the whole to which it belongs. For this whole is unique; there is but one universe, and therefore nothing else with which it can be compared. When we are examining particular things, we explain one fact by reference to other facts of the same kind. But we cannot in this way explain the universe, because it is the only fact of its kind. Our view of it must be formed from itself alone and from the facts and relations which it includes. And this view will not be simply a description of our experience (for such would be endless), but an interpretation of it—an attempt to see the meaning of particular things in the light of the whole to which they belong. And the light which makes all things visible may be itself unfathomable to the direct gaze.

Thus, within the realm of thought, we may discover three lines of contrast all connected with one another: the contrast between transient and permanent factors; that between our apprehension of the details of experience and the intuition of the whole; and that between the precise and definite concepts of science and the ideas whose inexhaustible meaning produces in us the sense of mystery. All of these contrasts, as they are revealed in our experience, fall short of absoluteness—admit of more and less. Permanence is a matter of degree for a mind evolved as man's mind has been; the whole cannot be grasped without its parts, and the parts are always fitted into a surrounding context suggestive of a larger whole; while, apart from purely formal and abstract concepts, the object of knowledge is always suggestive of more than is definitely known. Yet, taking each of these contrasts, belief in God may be said to belong to one and not to the other of the contrasted opposites. It is not transient, but, in varying forms and degrees, a permanent characteristic of almost all reflective thought. In spite of the exuberance of polytheistic mythologies, its object nearly always stands in a unique relation to man's life and the course of the world as a whole. And, equally in spite of the most rationalistic theology, God, in our idea of Him, is almost always conceived as at once the source of all reality and the ground of all knowledge and, at the same time, as never fully comprehensible in His own nature. Thus it comes about that the idea of God does not present entirely the same features, as it appears in successive periods of human thought. The history of these changes, and of the development they show, has been made the subject of many works on religion and theology. No attempt can be made here to trace this history even in its later period, far less to give any criticism of modern writers on the subject. At most all that can be done is to bring out, in very general terms, the way in which the problem presents itself to the thought of the present day, and to compare it with the attitude of times immediately antecedent to our own. Every age has its own attitude to the theistic idea. This attitude is bound up with its dominant scientific conceptions, with its knowledge of nature and of history, and with its ideals. The idea of God may be affected by all these, and in its turn it influences and modifies them. However conceived, the idea is always unique in the importance and comprehensiveness of its object, so that our whole thinking and life tend in one direction or in another according as it is accepted or rejected; while, on the other hand, being thus closely associated with the whole mental attitude, the theistic idea is modified according to the kind of concepts which experience and science have rendered dominant in our consciousness. Further, these concepts commonly owe their place in men's minds to influences which are for the most part independent of theological belief or religious experience: so that, at any period, God is defined or described almost in the same way both by those who profess belief in Him and by those who deny or doubt His existence.

If we survey the question of theistic belief and argument as it appears throughout the times usually described as modern, we may, I think, distinguish three different attitudes to the meaning of the question and the methods appropriate for dealing with it. Each of these is characteristic of a different period. It is not indeed peculiar to it; it persists after the time of its bloom, or it may be traced at an earlier stage of growth; and all of them may be found in previous history. Yet each flourished most abundantly in a particular period and is representative of the prevailing spirit of that period in things of the mind. They are thus the attitudes of different ages. The first of these ages may be called the Age of

Reason. It covered most of the seventeenth and eighteenth centuries; and we may look upon it as ushered in by Descartes and as brought to an end by Hume and Kant. In this period the traditional 'proofs' for the existence of God were elaborated and discussed, asserted and refuted. The next period may be called, in Kant's words, the Age of Criticism; it is founded on a limited distrust of reason, and it issued in the doctrine which became known in the latter half of the nineteenth century as Agnosticism. For this type of view, knowledge of God is not possible; but it is possible that belief or faith may still remain. These two attitudes—those of the Age of Reason and of the Age of Criticism—appear at first sight to be exhaustive. Either, it would seem, we must trust reason and follow it whithersoever it leads; or else we must distrust reason and avoid it altogether in subjects to which it is inadequate. But these alternatives do not exhaust the possible attitudes of thought. Reason was somewhat narrowly conceived in the period of rationalism, and the criticism that followed destroyed less than it appeared to destroy. Most of us have recovered from agnosticism without thereby reverting to rationalism, and in the present period of attempted reconstruction there are signs that this age may be destined to be an Age of Comprehension.

These bald statements need explanation. We may begin to understand the attitude of contemporary thought to the problem of theism by looking more closely at the way in which that problem was dealt with both in the period of rationalism and in that of criticism, so as to discover in what respects their attitude and point of view differ from the attitude and point of view which we are justified in adopting.

The outstanding feature of the first period—or of the Age of Reason—was the formulation and discussion of the proofs of the existence of God—proofs which had been handed on from previous thinkers, especially the Scholastic philosophers. From the presence of the idea in our minds of a being than whom no greater can be conceived, or of a perfect being, from the mere existence of the world, and from the marks of design or adaptation in its parts, it was argued that God exists. These are the well-known Ontological, Cosmological, and Teleological arguments. Then, as now, there were two sides to the argument. Some held that the proofs, or some of them, were valid demonstrations and that consequently we can prove that God exists in much the same way as we can prove a mathematical or physical theorem; while others held that all the so-called proofs are invalid, and that consequently God does not exist, or at any rate that we have no ground for saying that He does. These proofs have now, for some time back, fallen into disfavour, even among writers who defend the theistic view. Most thinkers have ceased to regard them as convincing and have even begun to find them uninteresting. The mental attitude of competent persons towards these arguments has thus changed in a radical manner from what it was two hundred or even one hundred years ago. What is the reason of the change? Most will answer with confidence that it is due to the criticism of the arguments carried out first

by Hume and afterwards more systematically by Kant.
Kant's criticism struck at the roots of the whole
rationalist method of thought, for he attempted to
show that, equally in affirming and in denying the
existence of God on grounds of reason, we passed
beyond the bounds of reason into territory over which
it had no jurisdiction. If his criticism is valid, the
' proofs' fall to the ground. But much more will fall to
the ground along with them: all assertions about
ultimate reality or the true nature of things will have
to be discarded. Thus not only the philosophies of
Descartes and Spinoza and Leibniz will be refuted,
but that of Hegel also and even that of Bergson. The
modern or neo-Hegelians, therefore, and the followers
of Bergson cannot really agree with the criticism of
Kant; and yet they have about as little respect as he
had for the old proofs for the existence of God. As
a rule they do not even think it worth while to refute
them, they are content to ignore them.

It would seem therefore that something more than
the effectiveness of the Kantian criticism is necessary
to explain the neglect into which the old theistic arguments have fallen. For myself I think that this neglect is not altogether justified and that the prevailing
temper of our age has dismissed them too lightly.
They do not indeed achieve their object, and prove
the existence of God. But they do show the inadequacy of the once popular anti-theistic views which
would explain the nature of all reality from the basis
of materialism or of naturalism. This, however, in
passing. The question is why we pay so little regard
to those arguments which a preceding age often

regarded as convincing and united in regarding as important. If Kant's criticism is not sufficient to explain the changed point of view, what was its cause? It appears to me that the true explanation lies in the special and somewhat restricted view of reason common to the Age of Reason—the view which we commonly name by the term Rationalism.

What then is Rationalism? Some distinguished authorities hold that the essence of Rationalism consists in this, that it is the use of reason for the purpose of destroying religious belief. This definition sounds as if it were the satire of an orthodox writer who was accusing the rationalists of prejudice—anxious only to destroy, not to construct. But it is not. It is the definition put forward by writers who count themselves among the Rationalists; and on that account it deserves attention. Yet, as a definition, it is faulty, because it does not bring out the characteristics of the rationalist method, only its purpose and result. And we find a method essentially the same when the purpose and results are of a different nature. If we turn to the great deistical controversy of the eighteenth century in England, for instance, we may, if we like, give the name of Rationalist to the writers on one side of the controversy, because their purpose and result may be said to have been destructive of the religious faith of the time, and refuse it to the writers on the other side of the controversy, because their purpose and result was the edification of men in the faith. But, if we do this, we overlook a fundamental similarity between the two sides in the controversy. Their reliance on reason, their view of reason, and their use of reason were essentially the same.   In these respects Butler and Tindal, for instance, are very much at one, however much they differ in the results they reached, and perhaps from the outset intended to reach.   The essential characteristic of the method called Rationalism was the precise but limited view taken of reason; and this feature was common to the writers of both camps.   They aimed at precision in their arguments and thus rendered a great service to clear thinking. But their view was limited.   By 'reason' they meant the passage from proposition to proposition by the ordinary processes of deduction and induction— especially deduction.   They brought to light what could and what could not be arrived at in this way. But they sought to apply to the interpretation of the universe as a whole the same kind of intellectual process as that by which one passes from part to part in the examination of finite things or from proposition to proposition in a chain of reasoning.   By 'reason' they meant reasoning—the work of the discursive understanding, as it is called, in contrast with that knowledge which partakes of the nature of intuition.

This distinction points to a very radical difference of attitude amongst philosophers, to which too little attention has been paid.   The first principle of Rationalism is, I think, put most clearly in the assertion or assumption of Descartes that "all knowledge is of the same nature throughout and consists solely in combining what is self-evident."   For Descartes and many other writers of his own generation and afterwards, mathematics and mathematical physics furnished the sole valid type of reasoning.   The

view has had a notable persistence, due to the certainty
of mathematical proof and the wide applications of
mathematical theory: though, in recent times, it has
been supplemented and, to some extent, supplanted
by biological conceptions. But Descartes, in spite of
his own biological interests, was so suspicious of other
conceptions than those of mathematical physics that
he gave a purely mechanical explanation of all living
things, except man, and held that the lower animals
were simply automata without any consciousness, feeling or life of their own. The fundamental experience
of his own conscious life made it impossible for him to
explain his own existence in the same mechanical way.
Indeed, far from doing so, he took this fact as the root
and origin of his whole philosophy. But, as he had
no immediate experience of the conscious lives of other
men and women, it is difficult to see why he should
not have explained their actions on the same mechanical principles as he did those of the brutes, and reduced
them also to automata. Huxley, nearer our own day,
went one better than Descartes. He held that all
human beings, himself included, were automata,
though automata that happened to be conscious. He
was a biologist, but according to his creed biological
conceptions had to be translatable into terms of physics
and chemistry; and so, under the supposed guidance
of the physical postulate of the conservation of energy,
he discarded his immediate experience of conscious
agency as something otiose and misleading—otiose in
so far as it was conscious, misleading in so far as it
bore witness to the real efficiency of the conscious
person in his environment. Thus may a theory lead

one to deny or discredit facts of experience which are more fundamental and certain than any theory. It is not theology or metaphysics only that a theory of this sort may exclude, but truths of any kind which concern a different region of experience from that in which the theory had its origin. The view that all knowledge is of the same kind throughout and finds its type and consummation in mathematics leads to an *impasse* in the direction of theism, but also to misconception in other fields such as psychology and history.

When reason is limited in this way and identified with the mode of reasoning appropriate to certain special subjects, doubt or discredit is thrown upon other subjects which had formerly been included in the realm of knowledge. Rationalism becomes restricted to definite topics; to all other topics the attitude becomes one of distrust in the power of reason. Thus the Age of Reason passes over into what has been called the Age of Criticism. The term is taken from Kant. But Great Britain and France, as well as Germany, have their prominent representatives of this attitude. In Great Britain it is represented by Hume and called Scepticism; in Germany by Kant and called Criticism; and in France by Comte who gave it the name of Positivism. In spite of many differences between them, all three agree in restricting knowledge within certain defined limits, with an unknown beyond. And Huxley has acted as godfather to the whole movement and named it Agnosticism.

Hume, the earliest of the writers named, though he did not use the term, expressed the essence of the attitude. Witness the last paragraph of his *Enquiry concerning Human Understanding*: "When we run over our libraries, persuaded of these principles, what havoc must we make? If we take in our hand any volume of divinity or school metaphysics, for instance, let us ask, *Does it contain any abstract reasoning concerning quantity or number?* No. *Does it contain any experimental reasoning concerning matter of fact and existence?* No. Commit it then to the flames: for it can contain nothing but sophistry and illusion." Here we have a deliberate attempt to mark the boundaries of the knowable—to draw a line with knowledge on the one side and only "sophistry and illusion" on the other. This is the common mark of all agnosticism, whether called by the name of scepticism or criticism or positivism. Hume is in a way more generous than Descartes: for he had two types of knowledge or ways of knowing—the mathematical and the experimental—whereas Descartes assimilated the whole process of knowledge to one kind—the mathematical. Hume gives us two kinds of science: an abstract deductive science which, however, can deal only with quantity and number and is equivalent to mathematics—or portions of mathematics; and an inductive experimental science which deals with matters of fact or existence. These remain; who need lament over the absence of the sophistical and illusory sciences of divinity and school metaphysics? They are shorn lambs; but the wind of Hume's criticism is not tempered to them. It is only the sturdy warm-fleeced members of the flock that he protects from its blast. He holds the winds of criticism in a bag and releases them at his good pleasure. If he had let them loose impartially, natural science could not have withstood the tempest any more than theology. For he has shown elsewhere that the experimental sciences depend upon principles (such as that of causality) which experimental reasoning does not justify and which are not founded on abstract reasoning concerning quantity or number. If Hume is right, all the volumes of natural science must go into the same fire as the works of divinity, and the greater part, if not the whole, of mathematical treatises will be scorched by the flame.

Hume's principles had the defect that they were destructive of all knowledge, not merely of theology. But, apart from this inconsistency, which is distinctive of Hume, the agnostic is always in difficulty when he attempts to draw the line between the knowable and the unknowable. He cannot mark off any region as unknowable, except on the ground of some characteristics which it possesses distinguishing it from the regions which are known or knowable; and thus in the very act of calling it unknowable he assumes some knowledge about it. The truth at which he is aiming would seem to be that all knowledge is *not* of the same kind. And this truth is sometimes indicated if not expressed by Kant and his followers in the contention that they abolish knowledge of God in order to make room for faith in Him, or that what cannot be known yet may be and even ought to be believed. When belief is further ranked by these thinkers among cognitive powers, it would appear that an idea of God, or an idea of the world as a whole, is legitimate, only it must be formed in a different way from our cognitions of particular objects in the world. Much the same may be said of Spencer's attitude. When he supplements his agnosticism by declaring that we have nevertheless an indefinite consciousness of the Unknowable and even describes this unknowable as a power and as tending to goodness, we see that his distinction between definite consciousness and indefinite consciousness is not so deep as to justify him in calling the one knowledge, and the object of the other unknowable.

In this way the agnostic attitude points beyond itself. It also suggests a supplement to that single line of thought which characterised rationalism. What is needed is a more comprehensive view of the objects and nature of knowledge than was attained either by the Age of Reason or by the Age of Criticism, and the time is ripe for an Age of Comprehension. Many great writers of earlier times have anticipated this more comprehensive attitude. Beyond the arguments which gave connectedness to their systems, beyond their 'positive' knowledge of scientific details, they had a view of the whole and were prepared to justify it.

What is it, asked William James, that chiefly interests us in a great thinker? And he answered that it is not his arguments but his vision, what he sees in the world or what he sees the world as being, not the logical steps by which he may profess to have reached that vision. The vision is more, and more permanent, than the scientific apparatus by which it is defended. This distinction points to that radical difference of attitude amongst philosophers, to which reference has already been made, and which is of fundamental importance for theistic thought. Some thinkers, as we have found, hold with Descartes that all knowledge is of the same nature throughout, and take as their model the method of the particular science with which they are most familiar. On the other hand, amongst thinkers so diverse in many respects as Plato, Spinoza, Hegel, and Bergson, we find that a mode of thought usually described as reason or intuition is regarded as giving a more adequate view of truth than the discursive process of the understanding.

It is not necessary to enquire here into the exact meaning which these various thinkers gave to this contention. But it is worth while to show how something similar to that which they name intuition or reason (as distinguished from reasoning) is required for knowledge of any whole, and especially of the only complete whole—the universe. Scientific investigation—so it has been generally acknowledged since the days of Galileo—proceeds by the dual process of analysis and synthesis. And of these two processes analysis is regarded as the more fundamental. We must first by means of analysis get to know the elements of which an object consists, and then proceed to reconstruct it (or show how it could be reconstructed) synthetically out of these elements. That this double process is sufficient for many scientific and practical purposes there can be no doubt. But there are certain limits to its adequacy even for scientific understanding.

In the first place, owing to the complexity of nature, our analysis is always incomplete; it does not include all the elements that are there; so that the synthesis of these elements which we then proceed to form will give an incomplete view of the reality. The more artificial and mechanical a thing is, the easier is it to reach or approximate to completeness in the analysis; as it approaches life and mind the analytic process shows growing incompleteness. A child's house built of toy bricks can be easily resolved into its constituent blocks, and then these can be put together again in the same order as before. But in life and in mind we have unities which admit only of incomplete—sometimes only of conjectural—analysis: so that far greater difficulties are thrown in the way of a reconstructive synthesis. We cannot get all the elements of a living thing separately and then construct a living whole out of them; and we cannot get successions of separate ideas or feelings or the like, which are not mind but only elements of mind, and then synthesise them into mind.

This points to another way in which the combined processes of analysis and synthesis are an insufficient guide to knowledge. Theoretically, as we have seen, the analysis is never complete—never exhausts all the elements in the reality studied—however sufficient it may often be for practical purposes. But further, as we now see, there is another limitation: the conditions which determine the union of the elements into a whole are apt to be overlooked in the process of analysis. The essence of the whole as a whole cannot be identified with any of its elements or with all of them. It was on this ground that Goethe criticised those who thought that analysis was a sufficient guide to understanding:

> To understand the living whole
> They start by driving out the soul;
> They count the parts; but when all's done,
> Alas! the spirit-bond is gone.

The 'spiritual bond' is just that which makes all the difference between a collection of parts and a living whole. But neither in biology nor in psychology has it been found possible to isolate this spiritual bond and deal with it as an element in the whole. We cannot 'catch it' (as Hume would say) without the parts or 'perceptions' which are its content. Nor on the other hand can we understand them without it. It disappears in the analysis. And the consequent synthesis must share the defects of the analysis: for synthesis can only deal with the elements which analysis has disclosed.

Thus it appears that, if knowledge is restricted to the two complementary processes of analysis and synthesis, it has certain limitations which mislead us and thwart the purpose of knowledge. But is it thus restricted? In our ordinary traffic with things we are not always engaged either in taking a thing to bits or else in putting the bits together again. We have or possess the thing first as a whole, and may even use it as a whole. And the case of knowledge is similar. Before we can analyse an object of knowledge we must have an object of knowledge to analyse. We begin not with isolated elements but with an immediate consciousness of an object as yet undefined but awaiting distinction and definition. Analysis reveals it as a many in one, so that from the beginning it may be described as a whole, though our perception of its structure is vague and indefinite.

This view of things—or of a thing—as a whole has been called Synopsis, to distinguish it from Synthesis. Synthesis is the making of a whole out of elements or parts, of which the enumeration may be incomplete and the principle of union overlooked. Synopsis is the view of a whole, which is not dependent upon a previous analysis, though analysis is needed to bring its parts into distinctness and to discriminate their relations. It is with a view of this sort that knowledge begins; sense-perception itself is of the nature of a synopsis, for in it we are cognisant of a manifold characterised at least by continuity, although without the unity of a true whole; and we rise from this imperfect synopsis to views of reality or of portions of reality with more definite boundaries and greater internal clearness until we pass to a synoptical view of the nature of the universe as a whole. Not only in the final stage of this process, but in each onward step of it, immediate experience has to be supplemented and guided by the imagination. Imagination is necessary for every scientific hypothesis as well as for philosophical or theological construction; but in every case it has to be tested by its adequacy to explain the relevant facts.

This mode of knowledge, therefore, is not introduced simply to justify a foregone theistic idea. We find the leading example of it in the knowledge which each person has of his own self. The self is a concrete whole, a unity of many elements or factors; and the consciousness of self is the root example of the immediate experience of a whole. Here at least we have a synoptic view of an object, which may be elucidated and defined by analysis, though analysis can neither exhaust its content nor supply the place of the intuition. It is an apprehension which is immediate,

which is lived in the moment that it is known—
although it is preserved in memory and clarified by
reflexion. Into this clarifying process there enters
the analytic work of the psychologist. The special
sensations which form the medium of our connexion
with the outer world, the organic sensations due to
bodily conditions, the impulses and desires which
prompt to action, the feelings of pleasure or pain
which give tone to each changing state, the succession
of images, the connexion of ideas, the mode of thought
—all these may be described. But we are aware that
the whole is not told. All such descriptions are
general; they are not minute enough to render the
concrete individuality of our life; in every account,
however complete, some elements of the real state are
lacking; the analysis is never quite exhaustive. Even
if it is his own mental state that the psychologist is
analysing, he is aware that his analytical knowledge
falls short of his immediate experience; there is more
in his life than there is in his analysis of it.

In this respect, therefore, the immediate consciousness or intuition of self has more claim to be regarded
as a whole than all the elements taken together which
analysis has discovered in it. And there is something
else, of far greater moment, which the analysis must
always fail to give. This is more difficult to name:
for in naming it we are apt to speak of it as if it were
one element amongst the others. But it may be
described as the sense of life or the sense of self. This
is not one element amongst others, such as sensation
or impulse or feeling. But it is something through
which all these are—through which they have being.

And this also brings out the separate individuality of each person's life, so that my perception of the sound of these words (for instance) is entirely distinct from yours, even although the most perfect analysis may be unable to find any dissimilarity between their respective contents. Thus all the parts which the analysis distinguishes are really in a whole, and the whole is there in all its parts. The 'spiritual bond' is there, but the analyst does not notice it.

The idea of self is founded upon immediate experience of self as a unity or whole of conscious life. We do not approach it from the outside; we have inside acquaintance, because we are it. But our knowledge of anything else, even of other selves, has a different starting-point. It too is founded upon immediate experience; but this immediate experience can only be of the aspect or side of that other self which comes into contact with our own life. Our knowledge of other men starts from the same point as our knowledge of inanimate things, that is to say, it is mediated and conditioned by sense-perception. Hence, if we compare one's idea of another self with one's idea of one's own self, differences are apparent. Both are founded upon immediate experience; but in the one case the immediate experience is of one's inner life itself; in the other case it is only of the outward expressions of an inner life. And as in both cases we are trying to arrive at an idea of an inner life, the immediate data take us much further on the way to our goal in the one case than they do in the other. Data of sense-perception, not required for self-knowledge, have to be depended upon for knowledge of an alien self.   How then can we pass from these immediately apprehended external data, which we call the expressions of another self or mind, to an idea of that self or mind?   Clearly, it can only be done by using an interpretative conception, such as our own self-experience supplies us with.   It is by a kind of imaginative insight that we attempt to view the process from the inside as it is for the self expressed in it.   It is by imagination, therefore,—an imagination which depends on sympathy.

But one or other of two methods may be followed in this process of interpretation.   We may start from the various external data by which the other self is expressed and which our analysis has discriminated, and we may then seek to find for each distinguishable part in turn its subjective correlate—idea, motive, desire, emotion, or the like—and out of these put together synthetically some sort of idea of the other self as a whole.   This is one method of interpretation, and it is common enough; but it seldom leads to anything like complete understanding.   Nor does it avoid the use of interpretative conceptions, though it keeps so closely to the elements obtained by its analysis.   For each of these elements it has to seek an interpretation in other terms than those first presented—a mental meaning for the external expression.   For each discriminated portion of the external data a fresh reference is made to the mental side; and the resultant idea of the other person's mind or character is a composite product of these various interpretations of particular facts.   This is the method of synthesis.

But it is not thus that the man of sympathetic

genius understands others. He places himself imaginatively within the other's self; he seems to take the other's place, to see everything from his point of view, to think his thoughts and share his feelings and desires. The former and more conventional attitude starts with each external expression in turn, and from it tries to look inward towards what is happening below the surface. The latter attitude also has its beginning from the external expression; but the genius of sympathy consists in a swift change of point of view; the observer ceases to be a mere observer, and becomes in thought what he observes: takes his bearings afresh to suit the new position and looks at things from the other man's angle. In doing so, he obtains an understanding of the character and conduct of another which is impossible to the observer who restricts himself to noting each separate act and speculating about its motive. At the same time genius cannot dispense with evidence. His most brilliant insight is always of the nature of hypothesis: it has not behind it the immediate experience of what he seeks to understand, which everyone has in the case of self-knowledge. Consequently, it must submit to testing by empirical data—by the facts, old and new, which constitute the external manifestation of the inner life which is studied.

The more an object differs in its nature from that of the observer himself or of his immediate experience, the greater are his difficulties in interpreting it by this process of intellectual sympathy. Hence the risk of failure when we try to catch the elusive 'spirit of the time,' or to put ourselves at the point of view of children or prehistoric man, or to understand the mental life of animals. Here—especially in dealing with primitive man and with subhuman life—there is call for imagination not only to appreciate the different conditions of the environment but also to enter into the different modes of subjective or organic re-action. And, seeing that it involves imagination, the synoptic view of reality, or of any portion of reality, cannot suffice by itself to establish the truth of its conceptions. Its interpretation of things must be shown to be adequate by empirical tests—by its ability to give a coherent account of those facts which it is the business of the analytic understanding to exhibit in detail. This is necessary when we seek to understand any particular object. It is also necessary if our purpose is to form an idea of reality as a whole. Here we approach the problem of theism.

An idea of the world as a whole—whether theistic or not—must be in agreement with the facts of the world and must offer an explanation of them. But it will not be simply a transcript of these facts, whose detail is inexhaustible. It must attempt to view them as a whole by grasping their principle; it will be a synopsis. So far, in illustrating this synoptic method, I have dealt with certain finite objects. The objects selected have been those to which a being for themselves, and thus an inner life, may be ascribed; and it has been contended that, to understand them, we must seek to penetrate to that inner life in order to reach the principle of unity which makes into elements of a whole what, judged from the outside only, would be taken as separate existents among which certain regularities may be discovered. But it has also to be pointed out that these finite centres of being are not self-sufficient. Their content is not simply unrolled from within; it grows through experience and by means of interaction with the environment. No view of the finite individual can be adequate which does not follow out its connexions with its environment; no view can be trusted at all which neglects them entirely.

We start with the self. But the content of the self is due to experience. Paradoxical as the statement may seem, it is only the external observer who would think of regarding this content as mere 'mental modifications.' To the subject himself it has a meaning which points beyond himself, and, as it increases, it brings him more and more into relation with other things. The self finds itself in presence of surrounding reality, and has to make its way in it as well as to form ideas about it. It is confronted with something which is both an obstacle to its activity and also the medium through which its ends can be realised. It comes to recognise an objective order—or laws of nature—to which it must conform and on which it can depend. And it is conscious of itself as one amongst other selves of the same kind, all living in the same objective world of nature and law. There is no moment in its career in which it is independent of these other selves any more than a time at which it is independent of the external world. And finally the self is conscious of an objective order of values—expressed not solely but most clearly in the moral law—which determine for him what he ought to seek and to avoid and thus give direction for his life as a free agent.

All these are features in the environment of the self; and a comprehensive view of man must take account of him as a factor in this larger whole. Thus it is from himself and his place in the world that man rises to a conception of the principle which upholds the universe and gives it a meaning. What kind of synoptical view are we justified in forming here? It must be all-embracing, for we are concerned with our position in the whole context of the world; and, imperfect as our conception of it may be, it must be something capable of finality—independent of any further and fuller view. Theism is a view of this sort —an interpretation of all reality as the expression of mind. But we approach the theistic view in a wrong way when we start with a definition of God and then ask whether we may attribute existence to this idea and say that God is. It is because they have started in this way that the ordinary theistic proofs often appear so unconvincing. And in this introductory lecture I have been anxious to point out the other and better way. We start with existence—our own existence and that of the environment; and we have to try to form an idea of the whole which will enable us to understand it both as a whole and in the broad lines of its diverse manifestations. The universe in which we find ourselves is, in the first place, a universe of actually existing beings—in particular, of finite centres of conscious life, or of minds, like ourselves. These can find their explanation only in what actually exists. From the mere idea there is no way to being. What exists cannot be explained by the non-existent. In the second place, our world is a world of law and order. Things are connected by causal and other relations, which our intellect can understand and upon which our practical life can rely. The principle of all reality must therefore be conceived in such a way as to explain this order. Further and finally, we are conscious of an order different from the causal and other relations which connect together the actual events in the world. This is the order of values, and especially the moral order, which guides our appreciation of all that occurs and is fitted to direct our life towards the highest good. This last, the order of values, is often overlooked in the construction of philosophical systems and often introduced only as an appendix in theistic arguments. But it is really fundamental. Whatever else the world is, it is a world of persons; and persons cannot be understood simply by what they are or do at any given moment. Their's is a continuous life, a striving towards a goal, a search for the good. We must take account of what they are fitted to become and what they know that they ought to be. They do not attain the ideal at any moment; but they recognise nevertheless that the ideal has validity for them and that its validity does not depend on their recognition of it. It also belongs to the order of the universe, and it is not less objective and real because it is so imperfectly manifested in space and time. In the principle of all reality, therefore, we must find the ground for the moral order of the universe as well as for its natural or causal order.

I have spoken of this age as an Age of Comprehension; and the need for comprehensiveness in our world-view is brought home to us by this distinction between the causal and the moral orders, both of which have to be included in our view, in spite of their obvious and manifold conflicts in our experience. This opposition between the world as a system of cause and effect and the world as a moral order—a scheme for the development of goodness—presses hard upon every reflective mind in these days when an old civilisation is falling in ruins before our eyes. How can we speak of goodness as belonging to a world such as ours? To this problem I shall turn in the next lecture.

THEISM AND MODERN THOUGHT

II

Our quest is for a view of the universe which shall be comprehensive enough to include and explain all its aspects. We must take into account not only the region of fact with which sense-perception makes us acquainted and the laws of nature which we come to recognise but also the moral order of which we are conscious. It is true that there are many thinkers who deny to the last realm the objective validity which they are willing to ascribe to the regions of fact and natural law. They hold that moral law—and the realm of values generally—is relative or subjective in a way in which facts and laws of nature are not. The question cannot be fully argued here. But this much may be enforced. The appreciation of value is, in this respect, on the same level as knowledge of things, their qualities and relations. We have no more reason for saying that value is relative because it is appreciated by us than we have for saying that facts are relative because they are apprehended by us. If we take any particular moral judgment, as that this man, or this character, or this attitude is good—let us call it 'A is good'—then what I mean when I assert 'A is good' is not that I like or desire A or even that I feel approval in contemplating A, but that goodness does, as a matter of fact, characterise A. The assertion may be wrong or invalid; but that is its meaning.

It is, of course, possible to argue that this assertion, thus understood, and all assertions like it, must always be without objective foundation, that they are always based merely on subjective preference. But, if this line of argument be adopted, it is important to remember that it is on all-fours with the argument for the subjectivity of all knowledge—with Hume's argument that there is no objective connexion in nature, and that, when we say or think there is, we are simply misunderstanding the subjective routine of our perceptions. In both cases the question in debate is fundamental, for it involves the interpretation of primary experience. If we say with Hume that the assertion 'A is good' means simply that the contemplation of A gives me a pleasing sentiment of approbation, then undoubtedly we cut at the root of an objective theory of morality. And equally, if we say with Hume that the proposition 'fire causes heat' expresses, properly speaking, nothing more than a connexion of ideas in my mind, due to association, then we must with him deny the objective character of natural science. And the denial of an objective morality, equally with the denial of an objective science of nature, follows from rejecting the plain meaning of the primary judgments of experience.

Subjective knowledge of this sort is no knowledge at all, for it defeats the purpose of knowledge, which is to understand the world—not to understand our understanding. And subjective morality gives no knowledge of morality. For, if the meaning of the proposition 'A is good' is simply that the person who asserts it has pleasure in contemplating A, it will be possible for another person, who has displeasure in contemplating A, to say with equal truth 'A is not good.' That is to say, the same proposition 'A is good' will be true in one man's mouth and false in another's: in other words, there will be no such thing as moral truth. If this position be adopted I know of no logical ground for its refutation. It would indeed be impossible to find such, where the axiom of non-contradiction has been set at naught. But the point has to be insisted upon that this assertion of relativity or subjectivity—if it be made concerning knowledge at all—will apply equally whether fact or goodness be the object of knowledge; and it results in both cases from an interpretation of primary experience which is opposed to the plain meaning of the propositions which express that experience.

On this point I cannot linger longer. I have only attempted to indicate the reasons which justify the assumption that moral values—or the moral law—possess objective validity, and therefore belong to the universe which we are seeking to understand as a whole, as truly as the laws of nature belong to it. The argument which I am about to set forth assumes this; but it will not proceed from the principles of morality alone; it will seek to comprehend both nature and morality; and, in this respect, will be distinguished from what is commonly called the moral argument for the being of God. Moral ideas (it is assumed) have an objective validity such that reality as a whole cannot be understood without them. But morality is only one factor in the whole which theism professes to interpret. We cannot take it alone as something independent of all other features of reality. And if we do take it by itself we are likely to reach an imperfect demonstration of the being of God along this one line of reflexion. The same inadequacy of any single line of argument might be shown by examination of the three traditional proofs mentioned in the last lecture. They do serve to define our conception of the universe to which we belong; they bring out the insufficiency of any merely material or naturalistic explanation of it; but they do not compel the reason to acknowledge that the world reveals a being whom we may properly call God, and, in particular, they fall short of justifying the idea of the goodness of God. Only if the world is seen to be somehow good shall we be justified in speaking of the goodness of God.

The moral argument, in the form in which it is usually presented, is due to Kant, who thought that by it we could reach a practical certainty of the existence of God—a topic which the theoretical reason left doubtful. "Admitting," he says, "that the pure moral law inexorably binds every man as a command (not as a rule of prudence), the righteous man may say: I *will* that there be a God....I firmly abide by this and will not let this faith be taken from me." That is to say, the moral law, the inexorable fact of duty, requires us to assume the being of God, not as a speculative truth for explaining nature, but as a practical postulate necessitated by the moral reason.

Kant's argument is open to criticism; but it is

remarkable as the first clear statement of the truth
that no view of the world as a whole can be regarded
as well-founded unless it is based on the recognition
of the realm of ends, as well as of the realm of nature,
to which man belongs. The theistic belief, which the
pure reason failed to demonstrate, was, he thought,
demanded by the practical or moral reason. He
must have been aware, however, that it is in the facts
of morality itself—in the distribution of good and evil
in the world—that we meet the most profound difficulty for any theistic view: that every religion almost
has moulded its theory in some way to account for
these facts, and that some religions have been prepared to say that the things of time are all an illusion,
while other religions have been induced to admit a
second and hostile world-power, in order that by any
means, if it be possible, God and goodness may be
saved together. The moral difficulties in theism have
to be faced by each succeeding age. Perhaps no age
ever felt them more keenly than we do at the present
moment. Many writers of our own day have dwelt
upon them; they were incisively put for the preceding
generation by J. S. Mill; still earlier, and shortly
before Kant wrote, they were pressed home with un-
surpassed power by David Hume. I will quote some
sentences from his *Dialogues concerning Natural Religion*, which contain the gist of all that has been ever
said on this side of the question, before or since. "In
many views of the universe," he says, "and of its
parts, particularly the latter, the beauty and fitness
of final causes strike us with such irresistible force
that all objections appear (what I believe they really

are) mere cavils and sophisms; nor can we then imagine how it was ever possible for us to repose any weight on them. But there is no view of human life or of the condition of mankind from which, without the greatest violence, we can infer the moral attributes, or learn that infinite benevolence, conjoined with infinite power and infinite wisdom which we must discover by the eyes of faith alone....As this goodness [of the Deity] is not antecedently established, but must be inferred from the phenomena, there can be no grounds for such an inference, while there are so many ills in the universe and while these ills might so easily have been remedied, as far as human under-standing can be allowed to judge on such a subject.... Look round this universe. What an immense pro-fusion of beings, animated and organised, sensible and active! You admire this prodigious variety and fecundity. But inspect a little more narrowly these living existences, the only beings worth regarding. How hostile and destructive to each other! How insufficient all of them for their own happiness! How contemptible or odious to the spectator! The whole presents nothing but the idea of a blind Nature, im-pregnated by a great vivifying principle, and pouring forth from her lap, without discernment or parental care, her maimed and abortive children!...Epicurus's old questions are yet unanswered. Is God willing to prevent evil, but not able? Then he is impotent. Is he able, but not willing? Then he is malevolent. Is he both able and willing? Whence then is evil?...The true conclusion is that the original source of all things is entirely indifferent to all these principles, and has no more regard to good above ill than to heat above cold, or to drought above moisture, or to light above heavy."

How is it, we may ask, that reflexion upon good and evil should lead two great thinkers to such opposite results?—that Hume should regard the power behind nature as a life-force regardless of the fate of its offspring, whereas Kant holds that the righteous man is justified in saying "I *will* that there be a God"? The reason is that they were looking from different points of view. Hume, we may say, had regard only to the facts of what men did and what men suffered. His privilege as a sceptic, to which he often appealed, carried some disadvantages with it. He saw the struggle and the pain, the cruelty of the world and the havoc of life, and he hesitated to go behind the facts. Kant may not have shared Hume's view of the morality of nature; but he would not have been appalled by it. Even if a perfectly good deed had never occurred in the world, so he says, his position would still stand secure. He was not looking upon outward performance, but upon the inward law of goodness and the power it revealed in the mind which is conscious of it. His reflexions were not based, like Hume's, upon the measure in which goodness was actually realised in the world—as to that he would have been willing to admit that it argues nothing for the goodness of the author of the world. It was the idea of goodness, which consciousness revealed to him, that formed his starting-point. He was aware of a moral law whose validity he could not question and the recognition of which secured him a position above the play of merely natural forces.

Hence Kant's doctrine of the postulates of the practical reason. The moral consciousness carries with it a demand that reality shall be in accordance with it. And this demand requires us to postulate the freedom of man and his immortality and the existence of the one perfect being or God. We are therefore justified in affirming these as postulates of the moral life. These postulates are all implied in the moral law, but not all with the same degree of directness. Freedom is necessary in order that the moral law may work at all; the moral consciousness depends upon it so closely that its absence would deprive morality of its basis. Were man not free from the compulsion of impulse and desire, he would be unable to take the law as the guide of his will. The two other postulates are arrived at indirectly. They are not necessary for the bare validity of the moral law; but they are required in order to bring about a harmony between morality and the system of nature. The moral law demands perfect obedience from every individual, and an infinite time is required in order that the individual character, with its sensuous desires and inclinations, may become subject to the categorical imperative: hence immortality is postulated. The reign of law in nature is not the same thing as the system of moral law; and the agreement of morality with the actual course of events can be brought about only by a being who will make happiness follow in the wake of virtue and fashion the order of nature after the pattern of goodness. Kant's ground for postulating the being of God is therefore this, that without God our moral ideas would be incapable of realisation in the world. We ourselves are unable so to realise them—that is, to make the world-order into a moral order—because the causal laws which rule the world of experience are entirely outside of and indifferent to the ethical laws which constitute morality.

The being of God is thus introduced as a means of uniting two disparate systems of conceptions. The infusion of goodness through the non-moral or natural —its victory over impulse and desire and its manifestation in the world of interacting forces—this is the problem that calls for so lofty a solution. The two systems have to be connected externally because they have no common terms. One of them is concerned solely with the causal connexions of phenomena. The other is compelled to seek out their final significance in relation to the ideals which practical reason discloses. The peculiarity of the view is that the two systems—the realm of nature and the moral realm— are at first regarded as mutually independent; they are subject to different laws, and their manifestations are of divergent character. Yet the moral order claims unlimited sovereignty, even over the realm of nature, while nature proceeds on its way regardless of the claim. Reconciliation can only be effected by an external power, and God is the Great Reconciler. It would seem as if neither system by itself—neither nature nor morality—stood in need of God. It would even seem as if, had they happened to be in better agreement with one another, God would have been equally superfluous. It is only because they differ, and because nevertheless there is an imperious rational demand for their harmony, that a being is necessary to bring them together somehow and sometime; and in this Being infinite power must be united with infinite goodness. Goodness is found wherever there is a will in harmony with moral law; but goodness alone does not make God. Power is found in nature; but power alone does not make God. Now, for Kant, nature is a closed and self-consistent system; so is morality. Neither, therefore, proves God; but He is needed to weld them together; and the moral reason demands their ultimate harmony. Hence God is a postulate of the moral or practical reason.

The special form given to this argument is a result of the distinction of the worlds of nature and morality, each of which is regarded as a closed system having nothing in common with the other. But even Kant's own thought points beyond this first and abrupt distinction; and no risk of error will be run if we take for granted that the distinction is not absolute. The order of interacting forces may be a self-consistent system; but it is not a complete account even of the things which form the object of physical science, and it is not a closed system. Moral values, also—though their system may be self-consistent—do not form a closed system. They are manifested in selves or persons; and persons live in and interact with the world of nature. The causal system may, of course, be considered by itself; but the abstraction is made for the purposes of science, and is in this respect arbitrary: it shows only one aspect of the world. And moral values are another aspect of reality, dominating or claiming to dominate the lives of persons. We must regard the two systems, therefore, not as the orders of two entirely different worlds, but as different aspects of the same real universe. From this point of view the argument will have to be formulated in a different way from that set forth by Kant. It will be necessary to have regard not to a connexion between two worlds, but to relations within the one system of reality; and we shall have to enquire what kind of general view is justified when both moral ideas and our experience of nature are taken into account. How can we vindicate the position that the actual world is a moral system, or that goodness belongs to the cause or ground of the world? This is the problem; and, in order to solve it, we must be satisfied not only that the moral order is objectively valid or that moral values belong to the nature of reality—a position the reasons for which have been already indicated—but also that actual experience, the history of the world-process, is fitted to realise this order. To show this satisfactorily would involve an estimate of the detailed features of experience, which we can hardly expect to be complete or conclusive; but yet upon this estimate we must venture.

It is possible to regard the power behind nature in the way Hume regarded it, as a teeming source of life which is careless of the fate of its offspring. Or, to use another of his metaphors, if we look at life as a composition which (if it have any design at all) must be designed to produce happiness in every part, we shall be likely enough to say that the picture must have come from the hands of an imperfect workman —one of nature's journeymen—if from any mind at all. But behind this view lies an important assumption—the assumption that happiness is the chief or sole end of creation; and is this an assumption that we have any right to make? Can we even assert that happiness alone would be an end worthy of the artist? If we recognise the supreme worth of goodness, can anything short of goodness be the purpose of conscious life? And goodness has this peculiarity that it needs persons and their free activity for its realisation.

It is not necessary to accept Hume's idea of the vital impulse; but certain views of the world's purpose seem put out of court on any impartial judgment of the facts. The world cannot exist simply for the purpose of producing happiness or pleasure among sentient beings: else every sufferer might have given hints to the Creator for the improvement of His handiwork. Nor can we find refuge in the old-time conventional theory that pleasure and pain are distributed according to the merit or demerit of the persons to whose lot they fall. The wicked often flourish, and misfortunes befall the righteous. That the course of the world shows some relation between sin and suffering may be very true; but the relation is not a proportion that can be calculated by the rule of three. True, only a brief span of life is open to our observation; and, after the death of the body, it is possible that the individual life may be continued indefinitely, while it is also possible that it had a history before its present incarnation. The hypothesis is therefore open that a future life will rectify the inequalities of the present, or that we now suffer in the flesh for the misdeeds of a previous career. In this way it might be possible to vindicate the required proportion between virtue and happiness, vice and suffering. But are we justified in relying on a hypothesis according to which the unknown larger life which surrounds the present is contemplated as depending on a principle which the present life, alone open to our observation, does so little to verify?

Let us suppose that the present life is only a fragment of a larger scheme. The hypothesis is at least permissible, for our life bears many marks of incompleteness. We bring—if not character—at least characteristic tendencies with us into the world, and our life breaks off with our purposes unachieved and intellect and will still imperfect. But we may reasonably expect that the present fragment will bear some resemblance in its order to the laws and purpose of its neighbouring fragments and of the whole. If the proportion of rewards and punishments to desert can be so imperfectly verified in the rule of this life, have we good reason to suppose that it will be fully verified in another? It may be said that the rewards and punishments of a future life are intended for the guidance of our earthly career. But if reward and punishment in prospect are to be regarded in this way as a means for controlling conduct or training character, do they not lose their effectiveness by being left uncertain and even by being postponed?

There is, however, one point in this life where nature and morality meet. Every individual person has before him the possibility of achieving goodness. Other values and the opportunity for them may be distributed more unequally. The enjoyment of art and the cultivation of knowledge stand in need of material instruments which are not in any abundant measure at every man's disposal. But opportunities of realising moral values are not thus limited. They are offered in every sphere of life and in all kinds of material and historical conditions; for their realisation needs the good will only and is not dependent on circumstances. I do not say that the opportunities are equal, but they are always there: whatever the circumstances, there is an attitude to them in which goodness can be realised and the sum of realised values in the world increased.

These considerations seem to point to an answer to the question before us. The question is whether the facts of human experience, and the facts of nature as shown in this experience, can be brought into consistent relation with our ideas of good and evil, so that nature may be regarded as a fitting field for the realisation of goodness. In other words, do the facts of experience agree with and support the doctrine of the moral government of the world—an ethical conception of ultimate reality, that is to say—or do they oppose such a conception? The answer to this question depends on the kind of ethical view of the world which we put forward. If by an ethical view of the world we mean the doctrine that the creative purpose must have been to provide the maximum of happiness for conscious beings, or to distribute that happiness equally among them, then it is impossible to regard the world-order as a moral order. Hedonism and theism, once their consequences are worked out, prove to be in fundamental opposition. If pleasure be the sole constituent of value, then this value has been largely disregarded in creation. Nature has been very imperfectly adapted to the desires of man, and human passions have been allowed to poison the wells of happiness. We may try to get out of the difficulty by imagining a Creator of limited power and perhaps of defective foresight. But even human intelligence might have foreseen and avoided many of the ills which flesh is heir to; and no one would attribute a higher degree of understanding to man than to his Maker. If mind is really the master of things, then that mind cannot have framed the order of the world with a view to happiness alone.

If we take the other and common view that happiness is distributed in proportion to merit, and that the moral government of the world consists in this just distribution, then also it must be said that experience does not support this view, and that it can be brought into agreement with the facts only by the somewhat violent device of postulating another life which differs radically from the present in the method of its government. The view admits a value beyond and higher than pleasure; but it looks upon a due proportion between merit and happiness as the sole and sufficient criterion of the moral government of the world. And therein it displays a narrow and partial appreciation of moral values. It reduces the whole of Ethics to the notion of justice; it treats all individuals as simply the doers of acts good or evil and deserving therefor suitable reward or punishment; it leaves out of account the consideration that individual persons, and the communities of individuals which make up the human race, are all of them in the making, and that to some extent they are their own makers—fashioners of their own character.

An ethical view of the world in which these points are recognised will not be open to the same objections as before. For it will look upon the world as providing a medium for the realisation of goodness and not simply as a court of justice which distributes rewards and penalties. I do not assert that this more completely ethical view gets rid of all difficulties. But it does avoid that special difficulty, arising from the unequal distribution of happiness relatively to goodness, which forms an almost conclusive objection to the previous doctrine. And that difficulty has been more than any other, or than all others combined, the burden of lament and the parent of pessimism. The struggle and pain of the world are the lot of the good as well as of the evil. But if they can be turned to the increase and refinement of goodness, to the lessening and conquest of evil, then their existence is not an insuperable obstacle to the ethical view of reality: it may even be regarded as an essential condition of such a view. Account for it how we may, the fact remains that the heroes and saints of history have passed through much tribulation and that man is made perfect only by suffering;

> But he that creeps from cradle on to grave,
> Unskill'd save in the velvet course of fortune,
> Hath missed the discipline of noble hearts.

The character of a free agent is made by facing obstacles and fighting with them; it is not formed along the line of easy successful reaction to stimulus. Facile adaptation to familiar environment is no test

of character nor training in character. The personal
life cannot grow into the values of which it is capable
without facing the hardness of circumstances and the
strain of conflict or without experience of failure.
Herbert Spencer, in his own way, has preached adaptation to environment as the essence of goodness.
Only in a world where all surrounding circumstances
correspond exactly with human desire will it be possible for a truly good man to exist. A straight man
in a crooked universe is inconceivable, he thinks. But
the question at present is not the kind of world in
which perfect goodness can exist, but the kind of
world in which goodness can begin to grow and make
progress towards perfection. Perfect adaptation would
mean automatism. It would not be and could not be
a school of morality. It is even inconsistent with
morality as I have conceived it, which implies freedom
and the personal discovery and creation of values.
And I will hazard the statement that an imperfect
world is necessary for the production and training of
moral beings. If there were no possibility of missing
the mark there would be no value in taking a true aim.
A world of completely unerring finite beings, created
and maintained so by the conditions of their life,
would be a world of marionettes. They might exhibit perfect propriety of behaviour. They might
dance through their span of existence to the amusement of a casual spectator (if such may be imagined);
but their movements would be all predetermined by
their maker; they would have neither goodness nor
the consciousness of good, nor any point of sympathy
with the mind of a free spirit. Not such are the

beings whom God is conceived as having created for
communion with Himself:

> Friendless was the great World-master,
>   Lonely in His realms above:
> Called to life an empire vaster—
>   Kindred souls to share His love.

These souls have had their beginning at the lowest
levels of organic life. They must fight their way upward through the long stages of man's development.
In this progress thay have to attain reason and freedom, so that the good may be known and chosen:
until, tried by every kind of circumstance, they find
and assimilate the values which can transform the
world and make themselves fit for the higher spiritual
life.

Are we justified in saying that the imperfect and
puzzling world that surrounds us is an unfit medium
for the moral life—if this is what the moral life means
—or that it makes impossible the adoption of an
ethical point of view in interpreting reality? I do
not say that experience of the relation of natural
forces to moral ideas and moral volitions justifies of
itself an inference to a transcendent goodness at the
heart of the universe. The mere fragment of life
with which we are acquainted is too scanty to bear so
weighty a superstructure. All I have argued is that
it is not inconsistent with such a conclusion. But if
there are (as we have seen that there are) other reasons
for saying that goodness belongs to the ground of
reality, and that the realisation of goodness is the
purpose and explanation of finite minds, then the
structure of the world as we know it is not such as to

make us relinquish this view. On the contrary a view
of the kind is supported by the general lines of what
we know about the world and its history.

The argument has led to this conclusion, that the
events of the world as a causal system are not inconsistent with the view that this same world is a moral
order and that its purpose is a moral purpose. The
empirical discrepancies between the two orders, and
the obstacles which the world puts in the way of
morality, are capable of explanation when we allow
that ideals of goodness have not only to be discovered
by finite minds, but that for their realisation they
need to be freely accepted by individual wills and
gradually organised in individual characters. If this
principle still leaves many particular difficulties un-
resolved, it may at least be claimed that it provides
the general lines of an explanation of the relation of
moral values to experience, and that a larger knowledge of the issues of life than is open to us now might
be expected to show that the particular difficulties
also are not incapable of solution. Accordingly, it is
possible to regard God as the author and ruler of the
world as it appears in space and time, and at the
same time to hold that the moral values of which we
are conscious and the moral ideals which we appre-
hend with growing clearness also express His nature.
And through the idea of God alone can this harmony
of nature and goodness be explained.

The argument which I have worked out may
appear to have about it—I am willing to admit that
it has—a certain air of paradox. If we were asked to
state the strongest objection to the theistic view of

the world which is felt at the present time, we should reply without hesitation that it lies in the existence and power of evil in the world. The dilemma of Epicurus is still with us: if God wishes to prevent evil but cannot, then he is impotent; if he could but will not, he is malevolent; if he has both the power and the will, whence then is evil? If the world had been so constructed that only good appeared in it and no evil, then (it is felt) the theistic interpretation might hold; but it fails to account for a world like this of mingled good and evil. The paradox of which I have been guilty consists in taking this very fact of evil and founding upon it a theistic argument. Had everything in the world been harmonious, had there been no discord, pain or evil, had all actual events brought forth moral values and been examples of moral law, then it might have seemed as if, in our explanation of the universe, we need not go beyond this one universal law, at once natural and moral, which would be displayed by all things at all times. But such an explanation will not fit our world just because of the discord between nature (including man) and morality. Nevertheless the moral order, as well as the order of nature, is of the essence of reality; and the two can be harmoniously united in one universe only when the world is understood not merely in its present appearance but as working out a purpose—that purpose being or including the making of moral beings. Unless we interpret the world as purposive, we cannot find room in it for both the natural order and the moral order; and when we do interpret it as purposive, we must attribute an idea and purpose of goodness to the ground of the world: that is to say, our view will be an ethical theism. If the purpose be the production of finite persons who will freely realise goodness, we have reached a point of view from which it is possible to explain, in general, both the slow stages of, and frequent lapses in, their moralisation, and also the nature of the medium in which this moralisation has to be achieved. Epicurus's dilemma has left something out in its alternatives. It regards goodness as something that can be produced by compulsion. It overlooks the possibility that the will to goodness requires the creation of beings who will achieve goodness freely and whose freedom needs varied experience in order that it may develop into secure harmony with the moral order.

If we look at the theistic interpretation of reality from this point of view, we shall see that certain modifications have to be made in the doctrine of the unity of the universe as it is held by exponents of naturalism or of pantheism. In the first place, the time-process as a whole, that is to say, the course of the world, must be regarded as purposive. Taking it at any moment, we cannot say that it is perfect or completely expresses a divine meaning; that divine meaning can be gathered only from its course as a whole or from insight into the purpose which determines its course as a whole. And, in the second place, the finite persons, in whom the spiritual nature of reality is manifested, must be acknowledged as agents in the accomplishment of the world-purpose, as possessing a real though limited power of initiative and therefore a certain measure of independence. The time-process is the means whereby this freedom and independence are made contributory to complete ethical harmony or unity.

This ethical unity, be it noted, could not be arrived at in any other way, if it be true that the realisation of moral values requires freedom. At the same time, the attainment of this ethical unity, just because it requires freedom, involves in its process a certain limitation of the actual unity of the universe. From this limitation it results that it is illegitimate to take any and every particular situation or event, especially those involving human factors, and to say "here the divine is manifested," or "the perfection of the universe required just this act; anything else would have been inconsistent with the completeness of the whole." Yet this is what the pantheist and indeed every determinist must say. Once an act is performed, he must look upon it as inevitable; anything else would have contradicted the nature of things; to regret it or wish it undone is to quarrel with the constitution of reality; it is a sin against the holy ghost of logic. But unity thus understood ignores the moral factor. The ethical unity of the universe is a unity to be attained. It is not to be found here or there, at some point of time, but only in the realised purpose of the world. It has to be worked out by individuals who are both free and imperfect. They are not simply modes of God, nor can their actions be referred to God as their cause. As possessing in Himself the purpose, or an idea of the purpose, of the whole time-process, God must be regarded as transcending this time-process; as communicating freedom to the individual minds whose being depends on His, He must be regarded as transcending them also; for their actual volitions may be alien to His nature; and this possibility may force us to interpret His transcendence as implying self-limitation.

The central point in our idea of God is not the pantheistic conception of a substance of infinite attributes; nor is it the deistic conception of an external Creator or 'first cause.' Neither 'own cause' nor 'first cause' will express it; but—if we must speak of cause at all—then it will be 'final cause.' And 'final cause' must mean the purpose of realising goodness. The difficulty of the conception of creation is mixed up with the difficulty of understanding the nature of time; and with that difficulty I am not attempting to deal. But the notion of creation involves a more essential point than that of a beginning *in* time or even of a beginning *of* time. It involves the idea of God as the ground and support of the world—not merely its beginning—for without Him it would not at any moment exist. For this reason, while we may not see God in each natural event, we must yet look through nature to God and see His mind in its final purpose.

Nature has been spoken of as the medium for the production and perfecting of goodness in finite minds. This interpretation we must give, if the moral and natural orders belong to the same universe. But it does not follow that it will explain everything. It would be too proud an assumption to assert that the whole of nature, of which we know only the barest fragment, has no other purpose than this one which concerns ourselves. Omniscience is a foible against which the modest philosopher should be on his guard. What other purposes than this there may be in the wealth of worlds which people space, or even in the small world known to ourselves, we cannot tell; and, except as a matter of speculative interest, it does not concern us to know. The comprehensive cosmologies of Plato and Aristotle, of Plotinus and St Thomas, even of Schelling and Hegel, were suited to a pre-Copernican universe, of which man was the real centre and not merely the being most interesting to himself. On such matters the only safe attitude is one of provisional agnosticism. But these doubtful issues do not interfere with our interpretation of our own consciousness and reality so far as known to us. The certainty of the moral law is not affected by anything that may lie hidden among the unexplored recesses of the starry heavens.

The same conception of purpose which guides the theist in the explanation of the world of nature, must serve him also in his interpretation of the realm of finite spirits. They too must be interpreted through their purpose, and this purpose will be, as before, the realisation of goodness. But there is this difference. Nature is a medium only; *through* it the end is to be reached. But minds are not a mere medium: it is *in and by* them that values are to be realised: they must themselves attain these values and not merely receive them. To nature we can ascribe no power or freedom of its own; each of its operations must be regarded as prescribed for it. But finite spirits themselves either contribute to working out the world-purpose, or else oppose their wills to it.

The world as a time-process has a certain unity through natural law, but this law fails to account for the volitions of free minds; it has a further unity in the moral order which points to a harmony not yet realised. Complete unity of fact and ideal can only come with the fulfilment of the purpose of which nature is the medium and which has to be worked out by finite minds in free struggle and free alliance. But the purpose exists eternally in the divine mind; and in all goodness we may see a manifestation of this purpose. In so far as men strive for its realisation they are morally at one with God; in so far as they lose touch with this end they are morally at variance with Him. The old moralists who explained 'conscience' as meaning 'knowledge with God' gave a fanciful derivation of the word; but the idea which prompted the derivation was not far wrong. In the moral consciousness we have some apprehension of the value which gives meaning to the world and which has been interpreted as a divine purpose; and in moral practice we cooperate in the fulfilment of this purpose.

The theistic view of the world which I have set forth is definitely an ethical view. It was based upon the admission of a moral order in the world; and it issues in a view which finds the purpose of the world to be the purpose of a Supreme Mind, and which regards finite minds as attaining unity with this Supreme Mind not by the absorption of their individuality but by the perfecting of their character through cooperation with the divine purpose. This view has not been put forward on account of its religious importance. That is a side of things on which I have not ventured to touch. It is given as an interpretation of reality which takes equal account of existents and laws and moral values. And, as such, it gives a comprehensive and consistent view of the varied aspects of our experience. At the same time it is not contended that it solves all questions or that it does not raise problems of its own. The solutions it gives are for the most part general; they offer a principle of explanation rather than an explanation of each event in detail. If particulars are explained by it at all, it is mostly by the aid of the religious consciousness and the intimate communion with God which it claims. And the idea of an ethical unity, and of the relation between God and man which it implies, raises speculative problems on which I cannot even enter.

So these reflexions end on the same note as that on which they began. The old things are also the inexhaustible things. Each age must face them in the light of its gathered experience and every individual must look at them with his own eyes. But there will always be more in the vision than he can translate into logical formulæ. In history and in science—the middle regions of our thinking—fact or theory may be established on a firm basis secure from the ravages of time. But we cannot thus fathom the mind of God or understand His way in the world. As our experience widens or turns into fresh channels old solutions fail to satisfy and new questions are forced upon us. Always we remain seekers, pressing

towards the goal, yet content that the search only and
not the goal should be ours, upheld by a faith which
we fail to put into words.

> These things are silent. Though it may be told
> Of luminous deeds that lighten land and sea,
> Strong sounding actions with broad minstrelsy
> Of praise, strange hazards and adventures bold,
> We hold to the old things that grow not old:
> Blind, patient, hungry, hopeless (without fee
> Of all our hunger and unhope are we),
> To the first ultimate instinct, to God we hold.
>
> They flicker, glitter, flicker. But we bide,
> We, the blind weavers of an intense fate,
> Asking but this—that we may be denied:
> Desiring only desire insatiate,
> Unheard, unnamed, unnoticed, crucified
> To our unutterable faith, we wait.

[The best introduction to the vast literature of theism is the
work of Professors Caldecott and Mackintosh, *Selections from the
Literature of Theism* (1904). Among more recent books on the
subject, mention should be made of Professor Ward's *Realm of
Ends, or Pluralism and Theism*, and of Mr C. C. J. Webb's
Problems in the Relation of God and Man. The argument of
the preceding lectures will be found worked out in detail in a
forthcoming volume of Gifford Lectures to be published by the
Cambridge University Press.]

HUMAN FREEDOM

When we consider the grounds upon which our faith in human freedom rests, we may readily suppose that our freedom never would have been called in question except for the large inferences which have been drawn from it. What knowledge is derived more directly from experience, and what experience is so close and intimate? First, we have the consciousness of determining issues when we will; second, we have the sense of being responsible for what happens as if the disposal were within our control; finally, we endure remorse as if the issue might have been different. If, merely by willing, events happen; if our responsibility for them is the deepest and most persistent element in our personality; if only by sophistry can we rid ourselves of remorse or doubt that, as we knew to do good, we might have done it, what other knowledge can intervene between us and so close, so intimate an experience, and what argument has a right to override experience?

Psychology, moreover, depends more and more on the activity of will for all its explanations of mind. Our activity is the spring and remains the centre of consciousness; by the power to select from the world and set ourselves against its forces, we become conscious of self and of an objective world; by imputing our actions to ourselves there is maintained, amid all changes of body and mind, the sense of personal identity. What other experience has any right to assail such a position? Is not the way to have any right knowledge of the world to accept all experiences and seek farther for their harmony, and not hastily to reject one experience because of its seeming conflict with another? Still less would it appear that we have any right to call in question any experience merely because it conflicts with a theory: for what is the worth of theories unless they are an explanation of all the facts?

In this conflict with theories of the universe, however, the real interest as well as the real opposition lies; and so grave and far-reaching are the issues that we must be prepared to meet the attitude of the cautious Northerner who would not admit that two and two make four till he knew what use was to be made of it; for beyond question the use is very large. If the sense of free-will is an illusion and our actions are the outcome of mechanical forces, there is little reason for going beyond a mechanical system of the world; while, if action is merely the outcome of fixed character and motive, we need not go beyond cosmic process and a determined scheme of reason. Only if there is in man a spirit that goeth upward, manifested in a power which acts freely and creatively, have we any reason for supposing that a kindred spirit is the ground of the world; whereas, if we can determine freely our own ideals and impose our values upon the world, it is impossible to believe that the world from which we spring is merely mechanical and determined.

Because of these grave issues, we must, therefore, prepare ourselves to bring our experience into dispute and set it face to face with the large questions of the nature of things, even though we may in our own minds still cherish the view that no mortal ever does know enough about the universe to justify him in setting up any theory against any fact of experience whatsoever, and, least of all, facts so personal and near.

On scientific, philosophical and religious grounds this experience of our freedom has been called in question.

Science, it is said, opposes to this idea of fluctuating voluntary action the idea of fixed mechanical law. As we progress in knowledge, this realm of unalterable law keeps encroaching on what, in our ignorance, we took to be the sphere of freedom and arbitrary action. Therefore, we are justified in expecting, that some day this latter sphere will be blotted out, and, meantime, we can believe that it only seems to exist because science has not advanced far enough to show its necessity. The real cause of willing is the fixed mechanical cause, and the sense of willing which accompanies the action is no more its cause than the striking of a clock is the cause of its moving to the hour. Thus willing only marks the hour, while an action is determined by other and mechanical causes.

The philosophical argument accepts the reality of will and its issue in actual happenings, but regards it as determined by motive and character. How can we act, we are asked, except on the strongest motive? And how is the strength of our motive determined, if not by our character? Rational action, therefore, can be nothing save action upon our strongest motive as determined by our character. And if we could act in conflict with our strongest motive and unlike our characters, the result would be merely irrational.

The religious argument starts from the omniscience and omnipotence of God. If He determines all things in wisdom and power, how can we suppose that He either could or would permit casual interference in His perfect plan from finite beings acting freely after their own restricted vision and foolish desires? Is it not like supposing that Infinite Wisdom first made a perfect machine, and then allowed mischievous children to throw pebbles into it?

These difficulties have been emphasized by the war in acutely practical ways.

1. It has placed men within the power of vast forces of destruction, which leave them small, feeble creatures at the mercy of an unpersuadable might, in the grip of which they cease to be persons and become things.

2. Great masses of men are marshalled against each other, their side determined by broad, natural, unquestioned feelings of love of country, and they are under such drill and are moved by such external commands that all sense of individuality is submerged. Character counts, but in a simple, direct, unreflecting way, so that, to quote an apt description, "men in war are what they are, only more so."

3. Finally, war has always been a great breeder of fatalism, and in the crisis of its danger, every man's religion is apt to turn in that direction. Amid "the arrow that flieth by day and the terror that walketh

by night," dangers against which no purpose, foresight or skill avails, there is little choice between chance and destiny; and it is a great strength to be able to believe oneself safe till "one's number is up." Furthermore, the human causes of vast calamities are usually so inadequate that we seem driven to ascribe the evils to the inscrutable counsels of Omniscience, lest the world and all that is therein should seem to be at the mercy of evil and designing men. Is it not better to believe that a war like this is part of the Divine plan like the winter frost which is to issue in the crumbled soil with the bountiful gift of harvest?

Logically these arguments are mutually destructive. Mere physical law as the source of all action is not the same as action determined by motive and character; and neither is in accord with a fate fixed by Omniscience. Practically, nevertheless, and especially amid the forces of war, so vast, so destructive, so blind, they may be found confused together, and all dimly felt at one time, and reinforcing each other.

Much argument about freedom is the mere refutation of a view of freedom which is so wide that it refutes itself, a view, moreover, which no advocate of freedom ever defended. It is necessary, therefore, before attempting to deal with these difficulties, to determine more precisely the limits of the question. That we are free does not mean, as seems to be constantly imagined, that anyone, whatsoever his character, can do anything he likes, whatsoever his situation.

First, if freedom of will means power to determine our whole life in complete independence of the forces around us, we need only to consider how much there is in this earth over which we have no more power than if it happened in the planet Jupiter, to find it refuted.

Second, if freedom mean that we can act as we would in utter independence of our character and the motives life puts before us, we need only to recall the confidence with which we rely on some and distrust others, to know that there is no room for discussion.

Third, if freedom mean that our destiny is wholly of our proposing and disposing, seeing how our birth, our training and influences, our opportunities, our capacities, our dispositions, are not of our determining, but are wholly appointed for us, there can only be one conclusion, for such freedom does not exist.

First, the question of freedom arises only regarding actions the issues of which we have power to determine. Though they form only a small section of life, they may involve vast consequences. Thus we can accomplish nothing by trying to push round the ship, but we can bring her round by applying ourselves to the helm. Moreover, even in respect of the many things which are beyond our power, we can maintain a freedom of spirit, an unconquerable soul, which may alter the significance of every event in life for us.

Second, choice is limited to a choice among the motives before us. Much discussion has taken place on the question of liberty of indifference. When we have two equally attractive roads to choose from, and we fix on one, are we not confident that it was equally in our power to choose the other? In some way at least quite equal choices are determined. The will cannot be held fixed in one place by equal motives as a needle by equal magnets. The famous problem of

Burridan's ass which stood between two equal and equidistant bundles of hay till it starved, does not exist even for an ass. Nevertheless, the real question of freedom concerns motives with great differences in value which are based upon reasons of different quality; and the vital question concerns the power to do what is right.

Thirdly, freedom can be exercised only within the limits of responsibility for the disposition and capacities with which we have been endowed. All our actions are in some way in accord with our character, and the only question is, How do we act upon our character so that by the right way it improves, and by the wrong it degenerates?

Finally, we are in the hands of a mightier power than our own wills, and freedom is not the ability to override its decrees with success. The supreme question regarding freedom is precisely the question concerning the Supreme Might. If it is of mere fixed force, our whole relation to it is to be moved with its movement by a fixed necessity. If, however, it be a power we can in some sense describe as a Father, because it deals with us as with children, desiring to see us directed by our own insight, our dependence may not be less, but it will be mediated otherwise than by compulsion. The question will not be whether our freedom can exist apart from the fountain-head, but whether that dependence is in freedom and for more freedom, or merely by constraint and identity of operation. Little is won in life by mere hard resolution and isolation, and much by hearing our call and discovering our true place; but the insight to find our right relation to a free world would be the highest of all acts of freedom.

In discussing the Scientific, Philosophical and Religious difficulties we shall bear in mind, without further reference to the limitations, that freedom is confined to actions and attitudes of mind within the power of our conscious wills, is exercised by selection from motives according to the bent we give our characters, and can only exist if it is· in accord with the powers of freedom with which we must keep ourselves in fellowship.

I. The Scientific Objection is that there is no room for freedom in a mechanically regular world.

With respect to this position, we can only stop to ask three questions.

(1) Is scientific law such an account of the real world, as could justify us in saying that the world is all of necessity? Law is merely a description of certain uniformities to which we must attend, not because they sum up all existence, but because our minds are finite and incapable of coping with infinite variety. It is more than abstraction, but more only as we might discover the signalling code from many messages not one of which we could replace merely from our knowledge of the code. To say there is nothing more than scientific law, no living, changing, feeling, willing world, is, in that case, as though we should say that, because the signalling system is mechanical, all its messages must be of machinery. On the contrary, were there not vital human interests concerned, there would be no more science than signalling. In the study of science we may rightly lose ourselves in the

pursuit, but to forget the conscious purposeful activity and living human values of the scientist and the ends of freedom he would serve in his discoveries of the uniformities of nature, is just as sensible as to omit the eye from the science of optics, because, in attending to other things, it does not see itself.

(2) Does even the mechanical order which science displays in any way justify the exclusion from the world of the uses of freedom? A world built up of hard, elastic atoms, which evolve order out of chaos by impinging upon one another according to Newton's laws, satisfied minds much occupied with neat mechanical methods. But the atom has now opened out into a world by itself, which is large and complex enough to have an individuality of its own, and regarding our knowledge of which nothing more can be said than that it seems to be a complex force of the nature of electricity which no one can imagine to be a picture of ultimate reality. At all events the new idea of the atom leaves measureless room for the possibilities of the universe.

(3) Even if we began with mere mechanism, why should we necessarily end with it? If it becomes something more than mechanism, ought we not simply to say that there were unknown powers in it we did not perceive? Should we deny the potentiality of a chicken in an egg, because to our eyes it was mere stuff for the breakfast table? Moreover, the whole idea of an organism as formed slowly by mechanical means and then working with more varied functions as it grew more complex, by which the mechanical conception of life was rendered plausible, has now fallen into disrepute. The humblest living creatures

choose amid their environment and on that choice they act; and organisation follows function and does not cause the functions to operate as a machine works after it is made. Hence life is of the nature of mind from its humblest manifestations. It acts on feeling and by knowledge however dim and confused, so that we ought even in the lowest forms of life to discern the possibilities of reason and purposeful choice, rather than deny the reality of the higher because it springs from the lower.

II. The Philosophical Objection is that there is no room for freedom in a system in which will is determined by motive the strength of which is determined by character. Though determination by motive and character is according to ideas and values set before us, and has no relation to material causation which is only some form of mechanical impact, the plausibility of the explanation is largely derived from its resemblance to mechanical necessity. It is, therefore, important to remember that the resemblance is only superficial, and that action on an idea is on a quite different plane from action on impact, and that the application of mechanical ideas is from first to last misleading.

This will appear if we distinguish between impulse and motive. The English language, it may be, does not distinguish so precisely between the words, but, if we would think with definiteness, we must often force an additional precision on common words. By impulse, then, let us understand the blind force of appetite or passion; and by motive the idea of some good we seek. For example, few drinkers get drunk on the deliberate idea of the pleasure of being intoxicated. Usually they are driven by an unreflecting appetite to take one glass after another, till they are in a state which contradicts every idea of good they ever formed for themselves. By persistence in this course, they may cease to be moral persons, and become playthings of passion. But to act rationally upon any idea even of pleasure is not simply to go with the strongest impulse, as a boat is turned by the stronger oar, or the balance sinks with the heavier weight.

Even an impulse does not really act in that way, driving a man as a kick drives a ball, so long at least as he is a moral being. The drinker conceives himself, for the moment at least, happier drinking than sober and self-respecting. But action on motive still more clearly operates with some kind of idea of ourselves. Even if it be mere pleasure, it is not by any driving force from behind but on an idea of ourselves as pleased. If you decide between a cinema and a sermon, you, in the last issue, decide between ideas of yourself as being pleased or profited, in which case manifestly something quite different is at work from the preponderance of the strongest motive according to any mechanical operation.

This will be still more apparent if we go on to distinguish between our motives, especially between pleasure and duty. Some dim comparison of these motives may be possible, so that it might flash across our minds that we should be more miserable shirking our duty than doing it, but the essence of the imperative of duty is that it never should be weighed against any pleasure or profit. Loyalty to everything sacred in the world and in our soul requires the repudiation of all such comparisons; whereas, if it were a mere question of the stronger motive, reason ought to require us not to omit any consideration however trifling or unworthy. Afterwards we may say a man has great happiness in doing his duty, but the point is not what happens afterwards. The question is, what is the actual motive before action which moves the will? Surely it is contrary to all experience to say it is what will please us most! The idea of happiness does not really enter on either side, but we feel ourselves between the ideas of being pleased with passion's vehement but fleeting suggestion and being worthy with duty's calm but absolute imperative, between which there is no common measure which could enable us to say, the stronger motive prevailed. If we act conscientiously, we enter upon no such comparison: and if we are persons of experience as well, we shall know that nothing is so dangerous for the eternal verities and obligations as any attempt to ask ourselves what is our strongest motive. If by the strongest motive we merely mean that the motive which prevails must in some sense have become strongest seeing it has prevailed, we cannot be refuted, but also we are not saying anything worth refuting; for if we have power to make a motive strong according to our idea of ourselves as pleased or worthy, we are free both for good and evil.

The special character of freedom will be still more evident if we draw a third distinction—that between regret and remorse. The Necessitarians usually help themselves out by confusing the difference. When we think an action could have been different, we are told, that we imagine ourselves with our present experience and motives back at the point of time when, with other experience and other motives, we had to act.   There are such regrets, and when we bethink ourselves, we know, if we followed our best light at the time, that they are vain regrets, and we often discover that our reasons for wishing we had acted otherwise are worldly reasons, and that the end would not have been peace.   Such regrets may often be confused in our minds with remorse, but that is no justification for confusing in our investigations things wholly different in principle. Remorse only arises when, at the time, we knew to do good and did not do it; when duty stood before us as an absolute demand, and wê made it a secondary temporal interest.   Thus it is not a question of transferring our present experience to the past, but of a dividing of the ways which actually was before us. Perhaps there is no real question of freedom except between motives of duty which can be made absolute, and motives of pleasure which can be allowed to get out of hand.

But what does that depend on, we may be asked, if not on character?   Here we must draw a fourth distinction—that between disposition and character.

For what, we are asked, have we remorse, except that our actions show us to be bad characters?   The whole Necessitarian theory of responsibility indeed, is nothing more than that we are inevitably mixed up in our own doings, as for example a wife, though she cannot mend her husband's ways, feeling as if she had done wrong herself, is thoroughly ashamed, and afterwards keeps nagging at him, not that she thinks anything could have been different in the past, but as another terror in wrongdoing to warn him off it in time to come. The long and argumentative expositions do not, in the end, come to more. But the question is not whether this confusion is often made. The question is whether it should be made. Should we not say there is no room for remorse, none even for regret unless we knew to do good, and are assured that we might have done it? No doubt our characters were at fault, but how?

When we talk in this way of action upon character, we ought to say action upon disposition, for it alone is given us and upon it alone do we act in that way of natural consequence. But it takes no great knowledge of life to discover how worthless the best natural endowment may be in face of temptation and trial. One man is born with a charming disposition, so that he delights in cherishing kindly relations with everyone; another is born somewhat of a boor, and his fellow-worms are continually squirming as he treads on their sensibilities. But your pleasant friend is not at your side in the storm of disapprobation or in the thick mist of suspicion. That requires, not a man of pleasant disposition but a man of character. But what is a man of character, if not a man who, through the exercise of his freedom, has established his life on principle and not on pleasure or prudence?

If our actions simply come directly out of what we are, where is the place for this distinction, the most vital of all differences? What is character, if not something formed by the exercise of freedom in the teeth of our natural disposition, by doing our duty, not because we liked it, but because we ought? The heart of the whole problem of freedom lies in this that we can so act on our motives and disposition that we form character, that by every act our character improves, or that we may so act on our motives and disposition that in the end we have no character at all. We do not act merely passively out of character, as we might out of disposition. Such easy going with the strongest motive means submitting to the two greatest enemies of character—insincerity and ungirt loins. The qualities of freedom are sincerity and self-mastery, and the supreme question is, How do we so act upon our motives and disposition that sincerity and self-mastery increase in us or degenerate? Surely not by any kind of necessity we know. No doubt it is beyond our explaining, for, though we know how a dead thing is put together, we know nothing of how a living creature is made. Yet so far is it from being beyond our experience, that we should have no experience at all, unless we were conscious of ourselves as free persons standing up against both impact from without and impulse from within.

On that freedom alone our responsibility rests. But responsibility is the one unchanging element in our personality, making us from infancy to old age say, "I am I." Our bodies change, nothing remaining unaltered; our minds hardly recognise themselves after a few years; the disposition of youth has little resemblance to the character of old age. But, through all those changes, responsibility continues, springing from a freedom which abides in some deep and permanent essence of the soul, which the acts of freedom alone can alter. Hence even for political freedom, men will die, because it may be a liberty necessary for the exercise of their responsibility; but surely that is a rational action only if the free soul of man is greater than all earthly good, because it dwells in another sphere than the blind earthly necessities.

III. The Religious Objection is that there is no room for freedom in the world of a wise Omnipotence.

On no subject has more dialectic been expended, generally of a type that has no contact with reality, and by which nothing in the realm of actuality ever was decided. God, it is argued, cannot commit any of His creative power to finite wills and remain omnipotent. But it might equally well be argued that, unless God can make free beings and still rule His world, His omnipotence is restricted to mere mechanical management of things. "Pericles," Hegel says, "enjoyed the greatest honour given to mortals, that he ruled men who had wills of their own." Why should a similar honour be denied Omnipotence? Might we not rather contend that Omnipotence alone, having the power always to gain His end, however much power He committed to others, could have been justified in entering upon the experiment of creating an order by way of freedom and not merely of an inerrant necessity?

Further, it is argued, that even if God wished to create us free, He, being Omnipotent, should have been able to do it without any risk of sin or failure. In answer it may be said that, even if we suppose that

Omnipotence does not include the power to make black white, or expose us to risk without any danger, we still leave a very practical omnipotence; or that, even if that were within His scope, there might be very good grounds for creating a world where white is white and black black, and risks real hazards. Omnipotence is the power to do things, not a dignity which, as it were, would tie God hand and foot. An Omnipotence which could only rule by fixed scheme, twirling the universe, as it were, round His forefinger, able to do nothing except as He directly did it Himself, would be a very poor kind of Omnipotence; for when He was done, He would not have a real world, with real children in it, but a mere Punch and Judy show, with puppets pulled by wires. As they are sensitive puppets, history would be simply a very bad nightmare. What are we to say, for example, of this war, fought out by mortal men enduring agonies of conflict and wounds and death, and women and children homeless wanderers on the earth, and bereaved mothers and desolate widows and fatherless children, if it is all a mere spectacle for a Deity who has pre-arranged all the issues, leaving nothing really dependent for ourselves or others, on the endurance of free men for righteousness' sake? Moreover, it is surely too much to expect even Omniscience to be for ever interested in such a puppet show, where nothing is ever uncertain, and nothing ever really accomplished.

"I cannot see," Dr McTaggart says, "what extraordinary value lies in the incompleteness of the determination of the will which should counterbalance all the sin and the consequent unhappiness caused by the misuse of that will."

No one can see it, expressed in that way. Imperfect determination is no more a gain than a breakable thigh-bone. Yet such is the preference for a living thigh-bone over an unbreakable weldless steel tube that hundreds of men are willingly enduring pain to have their own bones patched up, however imperfectly, rather than have their limbs off and replaced by a less breakable substitute. Similarly the issue is not determination either perfect or imperfect, but a living freedom, whereby, at whatsoever pain and risk, we may attain to walking by our own insight after our own resolution; whereby in freedom, and not in slavery, we may in the end make truth our own and abide in a love our own hearts have chosen. Otherwise it is vain for us to talk of a real world, or to describe ourselves as the children of God. If, however, God has not only made us in His own image, but if, through the freedom we have, we must win greater freedom, if the truth of all necessity is freedom, if all freedom stands not by parliaments and other safeguards, but by the faithfulness of those who have discerned that freedom is greater than life, then we can see in all our struggles, not only the creation of God's children, but the creation of God's final order as something not imposed upon us, but as a truth accepted by our own insight and a love embraced by our own hearts. Then also we may see that freedom is not of mere hard resolution, but is the end towards which all God's appointments for us are directed.

THE PROBLEM OF THE EXISTENCE OF MORAL EVIL

The problem of evil is a standing difficulty for any kind of philosophy which regards the world as rational, or as expressive of purpose. It is a puzzle to others than theists or Christians; and neither theism nor Christianity called it into being. But the existence of evil is a greater crux for theism of any kind than for other philosophical theories of the world. For theism not only maintains that the world is an expression of intelligent purpose, but also that at bottom it embodies the purpose of one will, and that wholly good. How, on this supposition, we are to account for the world's evil, has been said to be a question that has received many replies, but no answer. It is certainly one of the most difficult intellectual problems which the theist has to face; and one modern philosopher of repute, at least, has confessed ignorance as to the lines on which a solution is to be sought. Personally I do not share the belief that the problem is thus hopelessly intractable. I cannot of course expect that the solution which seems satisfactory to me will commend itself as acceptable to all even of those who face the problem from a similar theological standpoint. Where the ablest of minds are commonly held to have failed, I cannot hope to supply an argument amounting to a rigid demonstration, or coercive of universal assent. I can but submit what seems to me to be the most promising way of attacking the problem, and aim at no more than bringing into association with one another certain elements in theistic, and especially Christian, belief, which we take for granted, and trying to shew that they carry us a long way at least towards understanding events in our world such as at first sight seem difficult to reconcile with faith in God as He has been revealed in Jesus Christ.

At the outset I would observe that the difficulty which theistic belief encounters in the actuality of the apparently incongruous element of evil, is always with us: it is seldom absent from the background of the thinking Christian's mind. If it be felt with especial acuteness in these days, it is because it has entered fixedly into the focus of our attention—in the case of many of us, perhaps, for the first time—in consequence of the physical and moral horrors of an European war. Recent happenings have not in the least aggravated the difficulty and complexity of the philosophical problem; they have simply brought it home to more individuals, and with greater vividness to us all. But minds are just now sorely perplexed; the faith of the very elect is tried and distressed. To the questionings thus excited within us, the answers seem far to seek; and some that have been forthcoming perhaps seem but imperfectly satisfying when found. Intellectual in their origin, these prevalent doubts and misgivings must receive an intellectual solution. In other words, it is to philosophy to which we must turn if we would overcome them.

In the two lectures which I have been invited to

deliver, I propose to deal separately with moral evil and physical suffering. I will not unnecessarily complicate our exacting subject by introducing an historical or critical discussion of the various attempts which professed philosophers have made to solve the old problems which beset it. As I have said before, I would simply lay before you, for what it may seem to you to be worth, the way in which, as a Christian theist, I myself endeavour in my own mind to meet the difficulties which the existence of evil, of sin and pain, presents to faith.

In the present lecture I will try to account for the existence in God's world of evil of the more serious kind—moral evil.

The fundamental theological belief which we presuppose is that God is Love. Now in whatever ways love, as attributed to God, may transcend and differ from the highest forms of love which mankind experience, we must be assured that divine and human love, like the divine and human spirits, have some features in common: otherwise it were useless to speak of God as love, or of the love of God. And, apart from all variable and incidental qualities which may belong to love as possessed by different orders of spiritual beings, we can, I think, say that everywhere and always love implies, firstly, self-imparting, self-communication, self-revelation. It is love in this sense that Christian theology has always assigned as the motive of God in creation. Further, love necessarily seeks the highest welfare of the being that is loved. The prayer "Thy kingdom come" may be regarded as one of the highest forms that the expression of man's love to God can take; the perfecting of the highest welfare of His creature must be the active expression of God's love for man. And if that highest welfare—welfare of the highest worth both to God and to man himself—cannot be promoted without entailing suffering and the possibility of sin, divine love—just because it is love—will not shrink from entailing such suffering. God will not spoil His child: He will chasten every son whom He receiveth, though no chastening for the present be joyous but grievous, if chastening alone secure the peaceable fruits of righteousness. Once more, love implies self-limitation in respect of exercise of power, and self-sacrifice in respect of tranquil enjoyment.

On these three suppositions concerning the love of God I shall argue not only that divine love is not incompatible with the actual existence of moral evil in the world; but also that in a world of the type to which ours belongs—a finite and a developing or evolutionary moral order—the *possibility* of moral evil is logically inevitable, while such a world may be the best possible. Remoter problems here suggest themselves: why did God create a world at all; or why an evolutionary world, and not a world perfect at once? These questions are perhaps futile; but whether they be futile or not, they are, on our presuppositions, irrelevant to our inquiry: which is, given a developing world such as we actually find ours to be, is there any reason to doubt its being the best possible world of the evolutionary type—which it must surely be if it be due to an all-good God. Taking the world and the reality of its evil for granted, or as given in experience, can we still believe that in and behind the evil there is a soul of good; and that in so far as the world, as we know it, is due to God's making as distinct from man's mismaking, can we be certain that it affords no evidence of absolute and superfluous evil? So long as it cannot be proved that the world is not the best possible of its kind, the theist's faith will remain reasonable and unshaken; there will be no need to seek refuge from what seems to be knowledge by blindly relying on feeling or assuming incomprehensible love, as Browning eventually did, or by faintly trusting the larger hope, with Tennyson. I believe that we have no need to budge from rational faith, so long as we are both consistent and in earnest in our use of the two words 'best' and 'possible,' when we venture to uphold the theistic implication that our world, in so far as God is concerned in its condition, is the 'best possible.'

What then, firstly, are we to mean by 'best'? What is the criterion of the good such as can be attributed to a world? In what sense can God and man alike say of a world that it is good? Good implies worth of some sort, and 'best'—in this connexion— for the theist at least, can only mean 'of the highest worth.' Now the highest worth is moral worth. That is an universal human judgment wherever moral judgment is possible; and it is an immediate moral judgment which we cannot go behind. It must be the judgment of God and man alike; else it is idle to talk of God. And we must play fast and not loose with it. It is just because the theist in his doubts and misgivings, and the atheist and pessimist in their attacks on theism, play both fast and loose with it,

that their misgivings and their gibes respectively
acquire the semblance of plausibility. For when men
allow themselves to "charge God foolishly," they
invariably forget this meaning of 'best,' and substitute
for it that of 'happiest,' in the sense of 'pleasantest,'
or hedonically the 'most enjoyable.' Certainly, in
this sense, our world is not the best—the happiest
that the human heart can conceive. Equally certainly, the theist must maintain, it was not meant
to be. If it were, it would not be truly the best, the
world of highest worth. The hedonist theory that
pleasure is what gives worth to life, the ultimate good,
the end to be striven for, is, I believe, nowadays
generally acknowledged to be psychologically untenable: for the Christian it is out of court. Happiness
may be a constituent element in the supreme end; it
may accompany the attainment of the highest end:
but the end itself, or the ultimate standard of value,
it cannot be. The best possible world, then, the world
that is worthy of God and worthy of man who bears
God's image, *must be* a moral order, a theatre of moral
life. Moral progress must be its purpose, its *raison
d'être*. Moral character and moral progress are the
best things in the world, and indeed the best things
there ever could be in any possible world such as ours.
To dispense with them would be to prefer a worse, a
lower, world. For unalloyed pleasure is condemned
by man himself as unworthy to be his 'life's crown';
and mere good fortune, unearned increment alone, as
we know, too often means degeneration. No pain or
want, no effort: no effort, no progress. *Necessity* is
the mother of invention; experience is the "becoming

expert *by experiment*"; virtue is achieved by the sacrifice, not by the seeking, of mere painlessness or happiness of the lower kind. Mere happiness would entail stagnation; but the law of God's world is moral growth.

We cannot have it both ways, then. The best possible world cannot be the most pleasurable; the most pleasurable cannot be the best. The best possible world cannot be the happiest while in the making; and it cannot be without its crown in finite moral agents.

The word 'cannot' leads us on to discuss our second leading term, 'possible,' with which again we are only too apt to play. Either 'possible' means something or it does not. If the word have meaning, its meaning must be different from that of 'impossible'; and 'omnipotent,' as specifying an attribute of the Creator and Ruler of the universe, cannot be used without absurdity to imply control over the possible and the impossible alike. It is, however, only by treating the possible and the impossible as alike for God, or by assuming that He must be the author, by arbitrary exercise of will, of possibility as well as of actuality, that the opponent of theism can secure himself opportunity to construct out of the existence of evil an argument against the existence or the goodness of God. This statement may seem provocative for its sweepingness and its dogmatic finality. But I utter it deliberately, and will presently endeavour to make it good.

Meanwhile it may be observed that the assumption in question leads to meaninglessness and absurdity.

There are two conceivable ways in which this charge
might be maintained; though as the one of them will
not carry the universal consent of philosophers, we
shall have to rely exclusively on the other. The first,
the argument of disputable soundness, is to assert that
the fundamental laws of logic, the laws, *e.g.*, of contradiction and of excluded middle, are valid independently of God and impose themselves upon Him
equally as upon ourselves, with necessity; because
they must be true of all terms and relations on which
thought, human or divine, can operate. If this be so,
we at once arrive at a distinction between the possible
and the impossible, necessary even for a Being such
as we conceive God to be: a distinction eternally
binding upon the Supreme Mind. And such a doctrine will perhaps not be unacceptable to common
sense. But, as I have hinted, such a view does not
commend itself to all philosophers. There are some
who hold that the valid, apart from the actuality of
which it is valid, is an abstraction, and a mental figment; that there can be no eternal prius of law—
even of the fundamental laws of thought, as they are
commonly called—external to the actual or to God.
Such laws, it is urged, like the empirically known laws
of Nature, must be grounded in, or be the expression
of, the nature of God, which simply *is* what it is: "I
am that I am." It is not necessary for us to discuss
this deep and disputed question as to the 'reality' of
the valid; for if we accept the view that the valid,
apart from the actual of which it holds, is an abstraction and a figment, and that the law of contradiction
is grounded in God and is not valid independently of

Him, we still have a sufficient answer to the assumption that the possible is an arbitrary creation of God, and that the possible and the impossible are alike to omnipotence. This answer is, that God is a *determinate* Being; not an indeterminate Absolute in whom all differences are lost. In that God is Love, *e.g.*, He is not hate; in that He wills a developing moral order, He does not will a paradise of angels; in that He is all-wise, He does not pursue the absurd. "I am that I am" implies 'I am not what I am not': not everything in general or nothing in particular. What is possible may thus ultimately be determined simply by what God is. But God *is* self-consistent, a definite or determinate Being; and that without diminution of His majesty or almightiness. In virtue of this determinateness, God is a limited God; but this does not imply that He is what we ordinarily mean by 'finite,' *i.e.* merely 'very powerful' as compared with us. Not to be a determinate Being, and not to operate by determinate means, are not, for the theist, derogations from almightiness. If any philosopher can think, without stultifying his reason, of so unconditioned an Absolute as a being for whom, and as to whom, impossibility is possibility, it is hardly our concern. Our God is no such Absolute.

But granted a God who is a determinate Being, a Being limited by the impossible and restricted to compatibility and consistency in action; and granted that His world is to be a developing moral order—the highest ideal of a finite world that we can conceive—then it must necessarily follow that there be the possibility, the risk, of moral evil in that world. There cannot be moral goodness in a creature such as man without the possibility of his sinning. Without freedom to choose the evil, man might be a well-behaved puppet, or a sentient automaton; he could not possibly be a moral agent. The highest or best possible finite world, we have seen, implies the existence of moral agents; it therefore excludes the puppet or the automaton from being the crown of creation. Were our conduct determined like the movements of the machinery of a clock, our world might manifest a pre-established harmony and fulfil the purpose of a clock-maker. It could not fulfil any ideal of its own, for it could have none; nor could it realise the ideal of a God who had committed Himself to the production of the best possible world. In both these respects a world from which moral evil was necessarily excluded would be something quite other than a moral order. It is idle, then, wistfully to contemplate the happiness the world might have known had the Creator made us capable only of what is right; to profess our readiness to close with an offer to remove our capacity to do wrong; or to indulge the wish that we had been made good at the expense of freedom. There is simply no moral goodness about a clock, however perfectly it may keep time. Freedom to do good alone, except after the gradual suppression of lower motives during a course of moral conflict, is no freedom at all. Such regrets, to which the ablest of men have occasionally allowed themselves to give expression, do but shew how difficult it is for human frailty to avoid that playing fast and loose with plain words, upon which I have already commented.

But now man, as a free agent, is a creator as well as a creature. His free-will introduces contingency —new possibilities. God stands "a hand-breadth off," as it were, to give his creature room to grow and act. And this implies another limitation in God: self-imposed limitation, motived by love. The actual world, the world of human society and human achievement, is thus due to man as well as to God. We are fellow-workers together with God in the realisation of the moral order: otherwise the world were no moral order at all. For the actual evil introduced into this order, man's will, not God's will directly, is responsible. Man's sin is not God's act. Doubtless God foreknew the possibility of human sin, and He is responsible for its being possible. But He is not responsible for its actuality; for conceivably it might never have become actual. God is never the author of our evil. He permits it, indeed, in order to have the good, or in order that we may attain the good: that is all. The goodness of God, then, in respect of the permission of sin, can be vindicated if we can convince ourselves that, from the point of view of both God and man, the moral order is worth the cost in moral disorder contingent upon it, and the misery which such disorder entails. So far we have seen that a moral order is the world of highest worth, the only kind of world worthy of God. Man's point of view shall presently be considered. Meanwhile let us clearly comprehend the logical necessity which links the idea of a developing moral order with the idea of freedom and the consequent possibility of sin. Freedom is the condition of "the glorious liberty of the children of God"; at the same time it is equally the human being's burden. We cannot have the one aspect without the other: such a demand is but the child's cry for the impossible, the self-contradictory. It is further a matter of logical necessity that man's evolution from the brute involves the inheritance of the basic springs of action which are sometimes miscalled 'propensities to sin.' These in themselves are not moral evils. They are metaphysical evils, if we care for that phrase: which simply means that they are not in the strict sense evil at all, but rather the necessary and non-moral ingredients of evolved human nature. These 'propensities' only become factors in moral evil when man, having passed from the natural to the spiritual being, wills to treat them in a manner contrary to the requirements of the moral law which he has learned. Morality means conflict, warfare, with the manifold temptations of the flesh which death alone can cure. God's almightiness cannot make this otherwise. But it is sometimes suggested to us that an omnipotent God could intervene with miracle to protect us from the severer forms of temptation such as occasion our most miserable acts of sin. I shall deal with this form of the appeal to God's omnipotence in my succeeding lecture, and will only remark now that the appeal implies that there is nothing God cannot do—even contradict Himself. In this connexion it clearly involves the confusion of the possible and the impossible, or of a Self-consistent God with an indescribable and indeterminate Absolute, of which I have already spoken. To secure immunity from moral relapse into the stage of 'ape and tiger'—as, for instance, in the case of the growth of Prussian militarism and its scientifically organised brutality—by promiscuous resort to miracle, would not only make the moral order a physical and intellectual chaos or disorder, but would also preclude that freedom which is the very essence of the moral order. The objection to theism on the score of physical evil is, as we shall see, that there is too much law or regularity in the world; the objection on the score of moral evil is that there is too much contingency in the world. And these objections are plainly contrary, the one to the other. Safeguards which would make us immune from temptation might secure objective right-doing, such as would possess absolutely no moral worth; they could not secure the morality which in the last resort is love—the only real fulfilling of the law—and they would not conduce to moral strength or moral character. Character is made, not born; and it must be self-made, not received ready-made. The developement of morality is naturally not continuous or uninterruptedly progressive; but to coerce it to be so would be to destroy its morality altogether. This may help us over a special doubt or difficulty engendered in many minds by the present war. Why, some have asked, does God allow such things to be? Why has He suffered a civilised nation for years to contemplate and prepare for a colossal war, for nothing but its own aggrandisement, and to the misery of whole races that had begun to hope that war might be no more: to apply its scientific knowledge and organising skill with cold deliberation to securing success by trampling on every gain in humanity that the race by age-long progress had acquired? To answer such misgivings we need to raise the counter-question: how could these things not have been, German minds being what we find they were? All has been the outcome of the free-will, and could only have been prevented by either coercion of freedom or suppression of temptation. Doubtless such intervention would have spared mankind much misery; and we cannot conceive God to be indifferent to human suffering. But what of the general question, of which this is a particular, if an appalling, case? Which is of the highest worth—the sparing of much suffering, or the permitting men to learn, in the only way they could learn, being what they are, that not in these ways is the culture of a people advanced? Suppression would mean surrender of the ideal which the world embodies; permission, only retarded progress towards it. And, once more, the morality of the race must be achieved at the expense of its happiness, not *vice versa*, when the two inevitably clash.

Thus, as I said before, the difficulties raised by the existence of moral evil are difficulties of an insuperable kind only on one or both of the suppositions, (1) that God must know no difference between the possible and the inherently impossible, and (2) that the best possible world must be a happy world, not a moral order. A world in leading-strings, as Professor Ward has observed, may realise *an* ideal, but can have *no* ideal that is truly its own—no moral ideal, that is. The Christian takes his stand, however, on the judgment that moral progress is the best ideal a world can have; that such is the ideal, for God and man, of this present world. For God to preclude evil would therefore be to do evil; to prefer a worse world to a better. But God is good; God is Love: and in comparison with love, omnipotence such as would exclude self-limitation dwindles into insignificance.

The moral ideal of our world, then, the ideal which is the world's own as well as God's, expresses the very nature of God.   And if the ideal be good, the process by which alone it is attainable is also good—despite the evil incidental to it.   But, we have now to consider, does man, with all his sin and all the misery consequent thereupon, acquiesce in this conclusion? Does his heart give the same answer as that which, if I have not argued amiss, his head should give?   If man fulfil the divine end in struggling, through many errors and many falls, toward the moral ideal, does he at the same time account himself to be striving for *his own* ideal; and does he deem the prize worth the cost, the end to justify the means?   Does he indeed think that life without moral strife would not be worth while?   I do not ask if all men think thus, for as a matter of fact they do not, or at least they profess that they do not.   There are philosophers, as we have seen, who base an indictment against the theist's God on the facts of human sin and suffering.   These, however, do so because they think God could secure His end without the means; not as a rule because they deny that morality is of the highest worth in the mind of man.   The hedonists who deliberately put happiness in the place of morality, and who accordingly ask

> What pleasure can we have
> To war with evil? Is there any peace
> In ever climbing up the climbing wave?

are nowadays scarce in the ranks of those who think at all. As for the many who do not think, and for whom the problem of evil has no intellectual existence, we are not now concerned with them. We inquire as to the verdict of the most strenuous and most thoughtful men, men who represent the race at its best—the race that is to be. And these, confronted with the choice between the happy and innocent life of the brute without thought before and after, on the one hand, and the life of moral endeavour, of moral tasks, of advance towards moral perfection, on the other, will, I believe, be found practically unanimous that a man may rejoice in that he is not a non-moral animal, but something higher:

> What were life
> Did soul stand still therein, forego her strife
> Through the ambiguous Present to the goal
> Of some all-reconciling Future?

The best thing in the world, I repeat, is moral character; the best possible world is the world which affords opportunity for moral growth. Even the immoral man recognises the supremacy of moral goodness; while the morally advancing man, from the standpoint he has gained, condemns any other sort of life than that of moral growth as incapable of satisfying his soul's needs, as unworthy of him as he now is. Had mankind never appeared, had creation stopped short of its crowning in a rational and moral species, the world's falling short of being a moral order could, of course, never have been known to it, and would have remained both unregretted and unapproved. The moral race which has willy-nilly come to be, although born to suffer, to endure the ills of this bitter-sweet world, nevertheless rejoices in living; approves the ideal of its Creator; accepts the chance of the prize of learning love; recognises that the attainment of moral strength and character is worth the inevitable cost: so long, at least, as it can believe the cost to be really inevitable, as I have maintained it is, and also that the evil be not superfluous or supreme.

This latter qualifying condition indeed needs emphasis, and it is now time to enter on its discussion. If evil were known to us to be ultimately insuperable, to be supreme over all good endeavour, to be purely, absolutely, and exclusively evil, in that it ministered to nothing but evil and were never subservient to the good; then truly the world might be in one sense a moral order, yet at the same time a mockery of man's moral aspirations. It would not then be the best possible world, the world of a good God: it would rather be worthy of a devil. So the theist, in order fully to resolve the problem presented by the existence of moral evil, must do more than prove that the possibility of moral evil in a moral order is a logical necessity, and that the actuality of moral evil is due to the will of man and not to the ('antecedent') will of God. He must also be able to repudiate the objection that his premises imply that possibly evil may be insuperable by God: by a God, *i.e.*, limited and self-limited in those respects which I have admitted, or rather insisted upon as essential to our explanation of the actuality of human sin.

Looked at from an abstract point of view, freedom in antithesis to external coercion, and contingency in

antithesis to external necessity, imply the possibility
that the good will never finally be realised, that moral
evil can ever assert and reassert itself, till it culminate
in anarchy. But this contingency that may ever
thwart God's purpose, considered apart from the
accumulated experience of the race and from all
motive, is an abstraction: a mere theoretical possibility such as logic-chopping delights in, if not a
nonentity. The theist is not concerned to maintain
that human volition is uninfluenced by character and
experience acquired in the past. If then moral advance, in spite of many relapses, should characterise
the future of mankind as it has undoubtedly, on the
whole, marked mankind's past history, there should
gradually be less and less possibility or probability of
final persistent opposition of finite human freedom to
the will and purpose of God. Bare possibilities, like
sheer impossibilities, must be given, in the discussion
of moral evil, no more substance than they intrinsically possess; and, as Leibniz said, "a naked possibility is nothing." Probabilities reasonably grounded
on experience, are another matter; and these the
theist may claim to have on his side.

For, in the first place, as I have just remarked,
moral progress has been made by the race hitherto.
Nor are we at liberty to regard this as a mere accident,
a state of things which there is an even chance of being
permanently reversed in the future. We have good
reason to believe, without appealing to God's power to
subdue all things to Himself, that in the long run the
good will be conserved, that evil will be exterminated;
or rather, will exterminate itself. I contemplate, of

course, an indefinitely long vista of time. There will doubtless continue to be grave set-backs in the moral evolution of man, such as that which startled the world with its self-disclosure two years ago. The discovery of the profoundest immorality beneath the intellectual civilisation of one of the greatest nations of the world, when we had been fondly thinking such a thing to be impossible, disturbed the faith of Christendom in the coming of the kingdom of God on earth, in the increasing supremacy of good over evil. We find it hard to acquiesce in the so slow grinding of the mills of God. This hard lesson, however, must needs be learned. Still, patience is not despair. The making of man may be slow; it may be none the less sure. God takes time. Nay, as Browning says, "man has Forever." We cannot indeed adequately discuss the problem of moral evil, from a Christian point of view, without reference to the Christian hope of a life to come. That belief may almost be called a corollary of our faith in God, when that faith is confronted with the fact of the existence of moral, or even physical, evil. The worth-whileness of life to the individual, who is called upon to suffer so much here while the race's moral progress is being achieved, receives a wholly new aspect in the light of this Christian belief in immortality; while the objection that the theodicy I am presenting seems to reduce to the identification of partial or individual evil with universal good, or ruthlessly to sacrifice the present individual to the race that is to be, is also hereby best refuted. If there have not yet entered into the heart of man "the things which God hath prepared for them

that love Him"; if premature death be but transla-
tion to another mansion in the Father's house, and
exchange of one kind of service for another; if "our
light affliction, which is but for a moment, worketh
for us a far more exceeding and eternal weight of
glory": then it is not enough to look only at the
things that are seen and are temporal when weighing
against the moral perfection of race or individual the
necessary cost in possible ills.

But, to return to this present evil world, I would
remark that the conviction that good will ultimately
prevail over sin is no mere sentimental interpretation of biological evolution. Purely organic evolution
seems to suggest no optimistic view of the world. But
man is not merely an organism, and moral evolution
is by no means determined solely by natural heredity.
There is a sense, however, in which survival of the
fittest bears upon the question as to the 'final goal of
ill,' if we remember that the environment now in
question, and the adaptation to it, are moral, not
merely physical or biological. It is something, surely,
that in human society as at present constituted, moral
evil can often only preserve its footing by disguising
itself under the name of good and resorting to self-
sophistication: witness the speeches of the German
chancellor. This false adaptation to environment at
least implies recognition of what the environment
really is.

Again, there is something inherent in goodness
which promotes the conservation, and something
inherent in evil which bespeaks promise of disruption
and extinction: contingency and free-will notwith-

standing. The wicked are like the troubled sea which cannot rest; the double-minded man is unstable in all his ways. The encroachments of wickedness, accordingly, are not consolidated. Its apparent gains are apt to prove vanity, or even loss. And it is plain that no universal conspiracy in evil is possible, such as should culminate in an anarchy of wickedness, a hell on earth. The intrinsic nature of human goodness, and that also of human evil, preclude any such ultimate defeat of the divine purpose. For the various impulses towards wickedness are lodged in different persons; one man wants this evil, another wants that. So evil desires and evil purposes conflict with one another; and evil, as well as goodness, thwarts and resists the conspiracy in evil. But if evil designs are inevitably at cross purposes, and therefore mutually destructive, there is growing consensus of the good. Conquests in moral goodness and truth, despite their temporary obscuration, once made, are made for ever. The world is ever the better for them, and knows that this is so. There is an unity of aim, a cooperation of purpose, a solidarity of interest, among men of goodwill. Tyrannies and despotisms, hoary prejudices and enslaving institutions, however firmly grounded on vested interests, sanctioned by self-complacency, buttressed by supine docility, or safeguarded by brute force and military power, have perished, are even now perishing, and will perish; but the moral law, despite its continual violation, survives and ever increases its dominion. Dominant evil is self-doomed to disruption; the good is intrinsically self-conservative.

Again, moral evil does not come out of good; but

good does come out of error and evil. Error and
heresy expose themselves, to the further elucidation
and definition of the truth; evil, in its very acquisition,
reveals itself to be the lesser good. We can rise not
only on the stepping-stones of our dead selves, but
even on wrongs received at the hands of others. Evil
learns by bitter experience that it is evil; and the
lesson learned swells the account of the good. Nor
does each new generation, or each fresh individual,
advance *wholly* by immediate and first-hand experience; though of course this largely is, and must ever
be, the case. For in human society social inheritance,
stored experience, counts for much. The higher the
moral tone of the many, the more difficult to realise
or to entertain, the more obviously evil, become the
evil inclinations of the few. For all these reasons
then, it is no flimsy optimism, but reasoned and
reasonable expectation, that, as history establishes
the fact of moral progress up to date, that progress
will maintain itself, nay perhaps proceed with ac-
celerated speed, in future ages: for the gains of the
good over the evil would seem to be cumulative. And
if this be so, the objection against the theistic conception of a self-limited God who has created creators
as creatures, that this act of His may involve the
final victory of human wickedness over the divine
purpose, largely dissolves away on consideration of
the tendencies inherent in moral goodness and evil as
such. There is no need to invoke divine coercion of
man's delegated freedom. On the other hand we are
not necessarily committed to the doctrine of universal
hope—of the perfecting or the salvation of *every*

individual soul. The souls of the hardened unrighteous —if any such there shall be—like the souls of the righteous, but in another sense, are in the hand of God. Whether belief in the divine justice, such as is knit together with our belief in a future life in the Christian insistence upon judgment to come, necessitate belief in a hell, in the possibility of lost souls, as belief in freedom uncoerced implies belief in the possibility of permanent evil characters here and there, is beside our present subject. But it seems to me that the problem of the existence of moral evil, the possibility of which is an inevitable consequence of freedom or of a developing moral order, however full of difficulties it may be, presents no insuperable obstacle to theistic or Christian belief if there be reason to hold that moral evil is no more to be deemed everlasting and destined to become supreme than it is to be considered absolute and superfluous, and therein inconsistent with a moral order, or a best possible world.

THE PROBLEM OF SUFFERING

In endeavouring to shew, in the previous lecture, that the existence of moral evil does not present insuperable difficulties to Christian belief, I represented that the position to which the Christian theist is committed is that in our developing world all things work together, as a whole, for good; and that the possibility of moral evil and the actuality of the consequences of such evil are the logically inevitable concomitants of the best possible evolutionary world. We do not maintain that all *is* good; that 'whatever is, is right'; that partial evil is not evil because it is the condition of universal good: nor do we assert that every particular evil is directly essential to the emergence of some particular good, or has its necessary place, like a dissonance in a symphony, in the harmony of the world as a whole. When we maintain that 'all things' work together for good, we mean by 'all things,' not each and every single thing, but the sum of things regarded as one whole or complex, the universe as a self-coherent order; and by the words 'for good,' we mean the highest good of the race, and of the individual *quâ* unit of the race—in a word, moral advancement.

It is by adhering to this same position that I would now face the problem presented by the existence of that form of evil for which human freedom is not necessarily, and often not at all, responsible: the physical and mental evils which are denoted by the words 'pain' and 'suffering.' Indeed any other position than that which I have just summarised seems to me to be obviously unsatisfactory and inadequate as a basis for the explanation of physical evil. In order to reconcile the suffering inflicted by the material universe upon mankind and other sentient creatures, with the goodness and almightiness of the Creator of the universe, it is quite superfluous, and at the same time wholly insufficient, to seek to shew that in every particular case, pain is essential to some special end; that every single instance of suffering may conduce to some particular good, or embody some particular providential purpose. To seek for a theodicy on these lines is as hopeless as it would be to-day to develope a teleological argument from particular instances of apparent adaptation, after the manner of Paley. But as there is a wider teleology than that of Paley, so there is, as I hope to shew, a wider theodicy than that which would base itself on demonstrations that, for instance, animal and human pain are sometimes prophylactic—a warning against danger; that human pain is sometimes punitive, sometimes purgatorial and remedial, and thus subservient to useful and benign ends. These contentions are undoubtedly true, and I have no wish to belittle their import. But by themselves they will not carry us far towards a theodicy. They do but touch the fringe of the problem; or, to change the metaphor, they do not go at all to the root of the matter. It is useless, again, to minimise the pain of the sentient world, or even to reduce our possibly extravagant estimate of it, except for the purpose of shewing that in spite of pain animal life is happy on the whole, and worth the suffering which attends it: otherwise a single pang of useless or superfluous pain is enough to raise our problem. It is faulty psychology, I believe, to maintain that pain is the necessary background to pleasure: a lesser pleasure would seem to be a sufficient contrast to enable the enjoyment of intenser pleasure. And if pain be sometimes stimulating, educational, preventitive, punitive, these facts are only significant for an estimation of the worth-whileness of sentient life. The knife may well be necessary to cure the disease; but why the necessity of the disease? The escape from mortal danger may require the painful warning, but why the mortal danger? Or, generally speaking, what are we to make of the remoter evil which renders the nearer evil necessary or salutary? Why the whole situation which calls for the particular painful remedy? The problem obviously lies further back than these particular and partial solutions recognise. Indeed we may go further and say that it is insufficient to argue that pain is a physical necessity. It must be proved to be a logical necessity; its non-existence must be shewn to contradict God's nature, or the necessary 'laws of thought,' as they are called, which are held to be grounded in the divine nature. This was the position which I took up with regard to the possibility of moral evil; and it must be resumed without substitution of any less general and fundamental position, if we would cope effectually with the problem of the actuality of physical evil. Short of proving the tenability of this position, we merely reduce the world to a clumsy arrangement, an imperfectly adjusted mechanism; whereas what we need to establish is that suffering is the logically necessary outcome of a moral order developing towards its perfection. In other words, it seems essential to a theistic or Christian view of the world, to be able to demonstrate that physical evil belongs at bottom to the order of what has been wont to be called 'metaphysical evil,' a necessary condition of a determinate finite world destined to evolve into a perfect moral order. And it would seem that this tenet can only be shewn to be false by a proof that some suffering, at least, is superfluous to a determinate cosmos intended to be the theatre of moral life. Our problem will partly be solved if we can find ourselves able to abide in the belief that no suffering which we experience is superfluous to the cosmos as a coherent system, however excessive it may be as a means to the accomplishment of a specific, particular, purpose, such as punishment or chastening, *e.g.*, may fulfil.

There will still remain, however, another question to be satisfactorily answered, before our theodicy can be complete. Granted that suffering shall have been shewn to be a necessary element in a world such as ours, it will further be required of us to establish the reasonableness of the belief that in spite of all the woes that man is necessarily heir to, life is worth while; or that though man is born to trouble, the glory of living is worth the cost.

Let us consider the former of these questions exclusively for the present. First of all it must be made clear that a world which is to be a moral order—and we are of course restricted already to the contemplation of such a world alone—must in its physical aspect be a physical order, a cosmos. That is to say, it is a logical necessity that the world be characterised by regularity or law. The routine of Nature which we have in mind when we speak of law may be variously explained. The spiritualist, who believes that matter is but the phenomenon of spirit, will conceive of law as another name for stereotyped behaviour, or settled habit. The dualist, who regards matter as existing independently of the mental processes of spiritual beings of any sort, will conceive of law as another name for the fixed properties or relations of matter in its ultimate form. This diversity as to the explanation of law or regularity, however, does not affect us. The theist, so far as his theism is concerned, may be either a spiritualist or a dualist. He is only concerned to shew that regularity or law-abidingness, whether it mask the behaviour of living monads (souls of some sort) or whether it be the impress exclusively of the divine will upon the determinate material system which He has called into existence, is the essential condition of rational and moral life in beings such as constitute mankind. The first postulate of science is the uniformity of Nature; and it is only because and in so far as Nature has been found to be uniform that she has been scientifically knowable. In 'science,' here, we must of course include common sense, or the common knowledge acquired by the race previously to, and independently of, systematic scientific methods as such. Probability is the guide of life. But without regularity in the world, there can be no probability about human life; no prediction, no prudence, no accumulation of ordered experience, no pursuit of premeditated ends, no formation of habit, no possibility of character, progress or culture—in a word, neither intelligent nor moral life. This is a most important consideration for our present purpose; it therefore needs to be emphasised, and its truth to be firmly grasped. It is not that, once pointed out, this truth is not obvious; for surely no one will doubt it. But it is apt to be lost sight of or ignored in the discussion of the problem of physical evil. Yet it is the key to the problem, if there be any key at all. Once let it be admitted that, in order to be a theatre for moral life, the world must be largely—I do not say entirely—characterised by regularity, uniformity, or constancy, and most significant consequences will be seen to follow. It will at once appear vain to complain, as some writers have done, that the orderliness of Nature is too dear at the cost of the suffering which it entails, and might well be more or less dispensed with for the benefit of the sentient and rational beings which people the world; for the reply is at once obvious that without this orderliness, this reign of law, rational life such as we enjoy would be entirely out of the question and impossible. And without rational life there could be no human morality. For moral life, then, the reign of law in the material world is a *sine qua non*. It is a logical condition of the highest good; and it is this in spite of the plain fact that it is not, in the broadest sense, an unmixed good —in other words, in spite of the fact that it is a source of suffering. We cannot have the advantages of a determinate order without the logically necessary disadvantages. These disadvantages, particular kinds of suffering, are not as such directly willed by God, as ends in themselves, or as particular means, among other equally possible but painless means, to particular ends. To make use of an old distinction, God wills them consequently, not antecedently. That is to say they are not desired by God in themselves; they are only willed because the moral order, which God does will absolutely, or for itself, cannot be had without them as means. Now to will a moral order is, as we have already seen, to will the best possible world; and it also commits the Creator, if the world is to be evolutionary, to a determinate world-plan. A definite or determinate goal and method of procedure, however, rules out once and for all any other possible goals and methods of procedure, if the law of contradiction be valid for, or of, the Supreme Being. The cosmical equation being defined, as Dr Martineau put it, only such results as are compatible with the values of its roots can be worked out, and these must of logical necessity be worked out. The possible excludes the impossible; all determination, as Spinoza taught, is negation. If two consequences follow from a given proposition, or from a given configuration of matter in motion, we cannot actually have the one consequence without the other; though the one may be pleasing or beneficial to man, and the other painful or in its immediate effects hurtful. Such a result by no means implies lack of benevolence or even of power on the part of the Creator, so long as power is not capacity to produce the inherently impossible; it simply bespeaks the inexorableness of the necessary laws of logic, or the self-consistency of the Supreme Being. That painful or hurtful events do occur in the causal chain is a fact; and it is thus, of course, that the problem of suffering emerges. That there could be a determinate evolutionary world from which all such events were excluded, a world of unalloyed happiness and comfort and yet a law-abiding or uniform world adapted to minister to the developement of morality, is a proposition the burden of proving which surely must be assigned to the opponent of theism. One can only say that in so far as we are enabled to pronounce on the matter by the experience we possess of the only world knowable to us, such proof would seem to be impossible. To illustrate what I mean here, I would remark that if water is to have the various properties which make it play the important part which that liquid does play in the economy of the physical world and the life of man, it cannot at the same time *not* have that noxious quality, the unpleasant capacity to drown us. The specific gravity of water is as much the necessary outcome of its molecular constitution as are its freezing-point and boiling-point; its thirst-quenching, cleansing, and all other beneficial, characters. There cannot be assigned to any substance such as water an arbitrarily selected group of qualities, from which all that may happen to be unfortunate from man's point of view are eliminated, and yet the world of which water forms an essential constituent be a cosmos knowable and calculable by the physicist, or even the plain man.

And similarly in all other cases. Mere determinateness—being this and not that—and comparative or absolute fixity of properties and behaviour, involve such and such concatenations of qualities, and not others. Physical evils follow with the same necessity as physical goods from that determination of the world-plan which secures that the world be a suitable stage for intelligent and moral life. The existence in the world of this form of evil, then, is no sign of lack of goodness or power in its Creator: it is simply a matter of compatibility of being and consistency of thought.

If this be so, then the disadvantages which accrue from the determinateness and regularity of the physical world cannot be regarded as absolute or as superfluous evils. They are not absolute evils because they are part of the order which subserves the highest good of man, or provides opportunity for moral developement; and they are not superfluous evils because they are the necessary outcome of that order. They are collateral effects of what in itself or as a whole is good because it is indispensable to the attainment of the highest good; they are necessary incidental consequences of an ordered, intelligible cosmos. They are not good; but they are 'good for' good, rather than good for nothing.

When dealing with the problem of moral evil, I observed that the attack upon theism took sometimes the form of asking why an all-powerful God could not shield men from the temptations which are the main sources of human misery, and so restrict the sphere of man's free self-determination. A similar objection is suggested by the occurrence of physical evil; namely, why does not God spare man much at least of his severer suffering by restricting the fixity of the course of Nature, and so eliminating the occasions or causes of our intenser and more grievous pains? In both cases the appeal is to God's omnipotence; and it is assumed that omnipotence means the capacity to do anything whatever, even the impossible. I have already criticised this appeal in some measure; but the omnipotence of God is so very important a consideration in connexion with our problem, that I will take leave to dwell on it a little further.

We need to recognise clearly that there are limits to omnipotence, if that word is to have any intelligible meaning. By 'power' we do not mean capacity to realise a contradiction, or to do the inherently impossible and unthinkable; consequently the term 'all-powerful,' or 'omnipotent,' cannot include in its meaning any such capacity. It is asking for the absurd to demand that God should make developing beings at the same time moral and temptationless. Similarly it is demanding the absurd to expect from God a moral order which is not a physical cosmos. It is not a question of power in God, but of incompatibility in thought and things. To save mankind from the painful consequences which logically flow from a determinate world-order, such as the earthquake and the pestilence, would involve the renunciation of a world-order, and therefore of a moral order; the substitution of a chaos of incalculable miracle for a cosmos ordered by law. The world must be reliable, trustworthy, regular, if rational and moral life are to

be possible in it, and man's reason is not to be hopelessly baffled or stultified. It is no question here of
God's directive agency changing particular sequences
here and there from what they would have been had
He abstained from such directive agency. This is
quite conceivable: quite consistent with physical
science, which does not *know* the material world to be
a 'closed system,' and therefore cannot affirm it to be
neither more nor less than a machine. It is in this
direction, doubtless, that we are to look for the
scientific justification of our belief in Providence and
prayer. Such introductions of new streams of causation, not calculable from knowledge of the past state
of the universe at different times, and not subversive
of its regularity, are quite a possibility for all but the
materialist. But the general or universal suspension
of all painful consequences of the world's regularity,
on the other hand, would abolish order from the universe and convert a cosmos into chaos; while the
suspension of some classes of consequences and not of
others, or the suspension of them on some occasions
and not on others, would beget confusion worse con-
founded. Man's reason would be baulked, his moral
confidence mocked. For if miracle were thus to be
lavishly introduced, where were its exercise to stop?
We should have to "renounce reason" if we would
thus be "saved from tears." Absence of pain from
a world such as ours, is in fact a two-fold impossibility:
it is incompatible with physical order; and, in consequence, it is incompatible with the possibility of
reason and morality.

Physical evil then must necessarily be. The further

question remains, however, whether any particular ills are superfluous. I do not now mean whether any particular ills are superfluous or excessive for the narrower purposes such as punishment, evoking of courage and patience, chastening of character, and so forth; I rather mean, superfluous to the world-system as a whole and to its general end of providing the conditions of the existence of a moral order. These are quite different things; and it is, I believe, only by considering this general end of the cosmos rather than particular possible purposes such as I have mentioned, that a satisfying theodicy is to be sought. The goodness of God is removed beyond cavil if it can be shewn that there is no reason to assert that the world-process involves more misery to sentient beings than is necessary to the attainment of the world-end. It is not necessary to shew that particular evils are not greater or more intense than human reason judges to be necessary for the production of particular salutary effects; and indeed it is very doubtful if this latter contention, on which some attempts at theodicy have been based, is tenable. This contention would seem to imply, moreover, that every specific form of suffering which man undergoes —the agony of tetanus or of cancer, for instance—is antecedently willed by God as means to particular ends; whereas, on the theory which I am presenting, it is admitted that many forms of suffering are not as such willed directly by God, even as means to high ends, but are simply cases of what in general could not but happen if there be a finite world, or moral order, at all. Now, that cancer and tetanus are divinely willed as such, is hard to reconcile with religion; and that excruciating tortures of these kinds are not excessive as evocative of fortitude and other virtues, can hardly be maintained in the face of human knowledge and experience. And, speaking generally, there is much more evil in the world, and some forms of pain and suffering are far more severe and intense, than what seems to us requisite to produce in men the virtues of fortitude, patience, self-control, and sympathy, which the enduring of pain undoubtedly tends to engender in many cases. There is again the fact that some human beings are born as abortions, imbecile in mind or insane, which seems to be quite inexplicable on the view that every form of suffering to which mankind is liable is a particular providence, an antecedently willed divine dispensation for the education and perfecting of the individual personality upon whom the affliction falls. Yet once more—and this is perhaps the hardest fact of all for human equanimity in presence of physical and mental evil— the distribution of suffering among individual men is entirely irreconcilable by us with any divine plan of adjustment of particular afflictions to the particular needs, the particular stages of moral developement, the particular circumstances, of individual sufferers. Even more distressing to human thought than the goading intensity of some kinds of pain and some forms of temptation, is the seeming utterly chaotic distribution of human ills. If we could trace the utility or purpose of particular afflictions, with their so various degrees of endurableness; if we could discern any kind of adaptation in quality or quantity of pain to the individual person's strength of character, moral state, need of awakening or of chastening: then philosophy might be able to agree with simple-hearted and simple-minded pious belief when it assigns a special purpose to every instance of suffering, and finds therein the visitation of an all-wise and all-good God. There are cases of suffering—perhaps by far the greater number of cases—which such a view would suit; there are some, however, as it seems to me, utterly irreconcilable with such a view. The wind is not always tempered to the shorn lamb; the fieriest trials overtake those, on the one hand, who need no excruciating torments to inspire fear or repentance or to perfect patience and trust already nearly perfected, as well as those, on the other hand, who lack the initial faith and moral experience to enable them at all to understand how severe affliction can be patiently endured for the soul's good or for the glory of God. And we know that sometimes, from apparent lack of such proportioning of burden to back, affliction altogether overshoots the mark and defeats the end which, according to the theory I am criticising, it should have been intended to fulfil. Sometimes the man who is minded to keep straight is hounded into sin; he who would fain in his last end be like the righteous becomes minded to "curse God and die." As the writer of Ecclesiastes says: "all things come alike to all: there is one event to the righteous and to the wicked."

I do not mean, in what I have been saying, to play devil's advocate, and to disparage the justice of God. The pessimistic utterance which I have just quoted from Ecclesiastes is perhaps after all a vindication of God's impartiality: and impartiality is a large part of justice. On the other hand, I believe the attempt which simple piety generally makes to explain human suffering by attributing it in every case alike to the calculated action of an immanent God, who wills the existence of pain antecedently, and allots every individual affliction to every individual sufferer—the attempt cannot save itself from logically issuing in just such an indictment against the divine justice. Nor have I spent time in protesting against theodicy of this type simply with a view to destroying a popular pious belief, or solely for the sake of criticising a theory which seems to me unsatisfying. I have said what I have said, in this connexion, rather with a view to offering to simple piety a staff, on which if a man lean, it will *not* go into his hand: with a view to securing acceptance of the positive theory of the relation between human suffering and the divine will which I was before presenting—a wider theodicy than that which perhaps the generality of Christian men and women unreflectingly adopt, and of whose insufficiency they are liable at any time disastrously to become aware. According to the wider theodicy which I venture to submit as a substitute for that commonly accepted, human afflictions arising from the relation in which we stand to the physical world are not willed as such by God at all: God does not afflict willingly (*i.e.* from His heart) the children of men. Physical ills are rather inevitable, if incidental, accompaniments of the order of Nature; they are logical consequences of the World-plan, if I may use a somewhat anthropomorphic expression, which on the whole ministers beneficently to man's good, and which is absolutely necessary if this world is to be an ordered cosmos such as developing human morality presupposes as a *sine qua non*. Physical evils, on this view, appear as inevitable by-products. They are not divinely willed in themselves, for any purpose whatever; they are, however, logical consequences of the cosmos or moral order which *is* willed absolutely by God, and the willing of which is due to the fact that God is Love. Now much of the evil which men are called upon to endure seems, as we have seen, excessive in severity, and superfluous both in quality and quantity for the special purpose of making the world evocative of particular forms of virtue in particular individuals. I have been contending, on the other hand, that perhaps no form of evil—neither the pain of cancer or tetanus, nor the affliction of being born with mind or body diseased, nor the devastating effect of storm or earthquake—is superfluous, that is to say a logically unnecessary element of the cosmos such as a moral order in general requires. It is at any rate for the impugner of theism to prove that some particular form of evil is in this sense a superfluity. Judging by such attempts as have been made, there is little hope of success for our opponent. And there is no more hope of success for attempts to achieve the wider demonstration that physical evil as a whole is a superfluity in a moral cosmos. World-building is generally admitted to be a futile occupation for men. If it be argued that the world might have been constructed with special reference to safeguarding the physical well-being of the human race, and perhaps of the lower sentient creatures as well, the arguer is unconsciously making two vast assumptions which in these lectures I have been endeavouring to expose. In the first place he assumes that an actual, determinate, coherent cosmos, in which the evolution of finite moral agents is to be attained as its goal or final purpose, can logically be possible without physical evil arising in it as the consequence of mere determinateness; and in the second place he assumes that even if this were a possibility, a cosmos without pain and effort could be a moral order, a highest or best possible finite world. The latter assumption involves hedonism, which, as I remarked in the preceding lecture, is psychologically untenable, and for the Christian is out of court. The former assumption is incapable of proof: it is only made to appear plausible by conjuring with the word 'omnipotence.'

If then it be granted that physical evil cannot be affirmed to be superfluous, it only remains for us to consider the second question which I said must receive a satisfactory answer before we can claim to have reconciled the existence of human suffering with belief in a God of love. This is the question whether physical evil, admitted to be necessary to the moral order, can be deemed by man himself to be not an excessive price to pay for the dignity of moral being and moral perfecting. For private evil to be justified, it must, as we have seen, be capable of being so regarded by its personal patient that he is not compelled to see in himself, as a sufferer, merely a means either to the perfecting of the race or to the realisation of the purpose of God. Man is an end for himself; and

Christianity proceeds, or should proceed, throughout its philosophy and its ethics on the basis of that truth. *My* evil can only be justified to *me* if the advantage accruing from it be *mine*: not humanity's, or God's. If my evil remain uncompensated to me, if the end do not for me justify the means, my suffering will for ever be a blot on the whole plan of the universe, even though the universe be the best possible world for humanity and for God. The whole plan must be necessary for my felicity, and my felicity must be judged by me as worth the cost I am asked to pay for it. It is not sufficient that there be a balance of the total of good or of happiness in the world over the total of pain and evil in the world; there must be such a balance to the good in every separate life, if the individual be an end and not merely a means to an end other than his own.

It will not be necessary to discuss at length the general question with which we are now concerned, because it has already been considered in its graver aspect—*i.e.* in connexion with moral evil. I could but repeat, now in reference to physical evil, what I urged in my former lecture. Man is certainly called to bear a grievous burden of suffering; but for the joy that is set before him in rational and moral life, he is willing to endure it. He clings to life even here; and we Christians believe in a fuller life hereafter. Believers in God acquiesce in God's purpose for the world; God's ideal is their own ideal also. It is the knowledge that God is fulfilling us, each individually, as well as Himself, and fulfilling us for ourselves as well as for Himself, that makes human life, in spite

of all its trials and sorrows, a thing to be desired. It
is just because a being so God-like as man, yet so really
of the earth, could not be moulded into the image of
God save from within his own self, by effort and suffering, that man accounts the payment of the price of
'the chance of learning love' inevitable. And, as I
have already observed, the balance of pleasure and
pain, of felicity and unhappiness, in the individual
life, cannot be struck so long as we confine our thought
to experience of the present world alone.

> Life is probation; and the earth no goal,
> But starting-point for man.

If it be that the special intensity of human, as compared with animal, suffering, be due to man's possession of his highest endowments and more God-like
attributes; and if it be, as Balzac observes, the thought
of the infinite that underlies all great melancholy: so
also is it in virtue of man's rational and moral nature,
and in man's thought of the infinite, that he can even
now realise that "the sufferings of this present time
are not worthy to be compared with the glory that
shall be revealed." Pain is indeed none the less pain,
nor evil of any kind the less evil, for that it shall be
compensated, or because it is a necessary means to a
definite end. But its hideousness is transfigured if,
besides being involved in the highest or best possible
world, it can be seen to have been "but for a moment"
in the time-span of just men made perfect. It is not
of the reality of evil, but of the worth-whileness of life
in which evil has a temporary place, that I now speak;
and in this connexion such thoughts as these are
relevant enough. I repeat again that the problem of

evil cannot be adequately solved by the theist, apart
from the hope of the life of the world to come. Without continued life beyond death, our ideals could not
be realised, our spirits would be mocked. "If I have
fought with beasts at Ephesus, what advantageth it
me if the dead rise not?" What advantage, indeed?
If, after suffering the hardships of earthly life—its
defeat of our purposes, its lacerations of our hearts—
in order to serve cosmic ends even though they be
divine, we went to everlasting death, we should be
instruments, not men; pawns, not children of God;
pessimism would be our portion, and God no object
of reverence and worship.

In conclusion I will barely suggest one thought
more. Man is liable to evils, I have argued, just
because he is a creator-creature, jointly with His
Maker actualising a moral order, a fellow-worker with
God. Perhaps this is not all, and the fellow-worker
with God is a fellow-sufferer too. I am unable to go
so far with certain theistic writers as to maintain that
there could be no spiritual life, no ethical attributes,
for God as well as for man, if there were no struggle
against evil, no enduring of pain; so that the existence
of evil is a condition of the life of God, and divine
goodness cannot be defined save in terms of evil.
That, indeed, seems to me a gratuitous and extravagant supposition in the light—or rather in the darkness—of our ignorance as to what God is in and for
Himself. But the evil of the world being there, one
cannot, on the other hand, believe God to be indifferent to it, or idle with regard to it. We must
rather believe that in so far as He can do so *without*

*cancelling the very conditions of the fulfilment of the
world-plan—the moral order as a whole*—God worketh
hitherto, and will ever work, to overcome the world's
evil. We must believe further, I think, that the
groaning of creation and the agonies of the human
race wring the heart of God, if I may so speak, and
cause Him soul-travail. This reflection is perhaps
not essential to the vindication of the Divine Goodness in the face of moral and physical evil, such as
I have been presenting. But as corrective of the
impression that rational theism contemplates a God
cold and aloof when it insists on our separateness from
Him, the thought will not be wholly out of place at
the conclusion of lectures which have necessarily been
characterised by the intention to follow exclusively
the cold, dry light of reason.

THE DOCTRINE OF PROVIDENCE

I. *The right idea of Providence*

It will be well that we should at the outset of our consideration of the doctrine of Divine Providence make sure so far as we can that we have formed a right idea of it—one that is both adequate and free from the disfigurements due to narrow interests, one that is in accord with the highest and best thought and teaching on the subject, one that is self-consistent and above all from a moral and spiritual point of view worthy of God.

We may approach this initial task by comparing the ideas of a 'general' and a 'particular' providence.

It has sometimes been held that the Divine Government of the world is in the form, not of the direct oversight and care of individual creatures and appointment of their several lots, but of such an arrangement of the forces that are to operate as shall tend on the whole to the punishment of wickedness and reward of virtue, and such a control of the strivings of the peoples and ordering of events as shall promote human well-being and secure in the end the complete triumph of righteousness. This may be described as the doctrine of a 'general' providence. It has commended itself probably to many who found it hard, and to whom it may have seemed almost irreverent, to trace God's Hand in the multitude and variety of ordinary and often seemingly trivial events, and who regarded it may be the majority even of human beings as too unimportant for God to concern Himself about their fortunes. This view of the method of God's Government may, also, perhaps be supposed to agree best with what Science teaches as to the operation of general laws. Moreover, it is a noble view, although it has little consolation to offer to the individual in his private cares and temptations and sufferings and losses. It is deeply instructive and inspiring to take long views of the world's course, and to mark the action of God in History, where in dramas which it takes generations to play out to their conclusion, it can often be more plainly observed than in individual lives. At this time especially religious minds cannot but be occupied with the Divine shaping of the destinies of nations, in connexion with the anticipations which it is natural to form of the effects upon the world of the present awful conflict.

It is hardly necessary for me to remind you that the Divine Government of the world under some of its broadest aspects is the constant theme of the psalmists and prophets of the Old Testament. While in the New Testament the prospect is held out of the full establishment of the Kingdom of God; and so we are led to regard all the great movements among mankind, and crises through which the world passes, as steps under God's direction towards the attainment of that great consummation.

But God's Providence, according to the idea of it

which has been and is commonly held by Christians, and which is taught in the most express manner by Our Lord Himself, is not confined to matters of wide significance, and the appointment of the results to be achieved through the operation of general laws. "Are not," He says, "two sparrows sold for a farthing? And not one of them shall fall on the ground without your Father; but the very hairs of your head are all numbered[1]." This saying and others like it lead us to think of the Infinite Mind as taking account of, and at least in some sense ordaining, every event. There is no distinction of great and little. Some things indeed—nay, many—cannot be held to be according to His Will, inasmuch as to a greater or less degree, directly or indirectly, they are evil. The world is in part a disordered world. Yet even the evil must be regarded as permitted by Him, while it is finally to be rendered nugatory in the working out of the Divine Purpose. So also every individual human being is the object of Divine Care. Our Lord's words were indeed immediately addressed to a "little flock" who had conformed themselves to God's Will and believed on Him Whom God had sent. But the whole effect of Christ's teaching is to reveal God as free from all partiality. This belongs to the very idea of the Righteous and Merciful Father, Who "maketh his sun to rise on the evil and on the good, and sendeth rain on the just and the unjust[2]." Certainly, also,

---

[1] Mt. x. 29, 30; cp. a slightly different form of the saying at Lu. xii. 6, 7; also at greater length, but to the same effect, Mt. vi. 25—34 = Lu. xii. 22—30 and 6, 7.

[2] Mt. v. 45.

we do not gather from the main drift of the teaching which Jesus is recorded to have given, that He led His disciples to look for any special favour from the dispensations of Providence in their individual lives, as regards worldly prosperity. On the contrary He prepared them for a lot full of hardship and suffering. And on the other hand, in a striking passage of His teaching given in St Luke, Our Lord warns His hearers against interpreting special calamities as indications of special sinfulness on the part of those on whom they fall[1].

Our Lord's sayings on the subject of Divine Providence form a characteristic feature in His teaching about God; they shew a striking advance upon the view of the condition of man presented in the Old Testament, "favoured," as J. H. Newman said, "with some occasional notices of God's regard for individuals, but for the most part instructed merely in His general Providence, as seen in the course of human affairs[2]." And although there are not in the other writings of the New Testament utterances on the subject of Divine Providence equally comprehensive and profound with those in the Gospels, the disciples had learned their lesson, and the general tenor of what they wrote is in harmony with the teaching of their Master. Such a view of Divine Providence is plainly not open to the objections which may be rightly felt to the applications which are often made of the doctrine by pious people, and by superstitious people who are not pious.

[1] See Lu. xiii. 1—5.
[2] *Parochial Sermons*, vol. III, Serm. ix on "A Particular Providence as revealed in the Gospel."

Owing to human self-regard men have been apt to put down as acts of Providence in respect to themselves any means by which they escaped from death or danger, especially if at the same time a number of others suffered; while on the other hand they have supposed that they could note indications of Providence, where they themselves have not been very directly affected, most often in calamities which they could interpret as judgments. The Divine intention in such events has been assigned in a grossly presumptuous manner.

The tendency to see God's Hand in exceptional, and especially terrible, events has been a natural one. And undoubtedly these arresting signs of God's Presence and activity have had and still have their place in the religious education of man. There are Divine 'visitations'—that is the Scriptural term—times when God makes Himself manifest, and thus seems to come nearer than at others. Though here too the lesson often most needed is that which was taught to the prophet Elijah. The Lord was not in the whirlwind and not in the storm, but in the still small voice. In any case the effect of Divine visitations should be to deepen a conviction that He is near even when we ignore Him. As religious knowledge grows, and faith becomes purer and stronger, we should more and more attain to a belief in His continual Presence. His Providence is one; it is continuous and unfailing. The term 'Special Providences' which at one time was in common use should be got rid of altogether. It can hardly help being misleading; indeed it implies almost necessarily a false, or at least an exceedingly limited and distorted, conception, suggesting as it does that certain events, affecting certain people, are to be regarded as in a peculiar sense providential. With such a notion the doctrine of a Particular Providence, an ordering of things by God, which takes note of all particulars, is as strongly contrasted as it is with the idea of a merely 'General' Providence[1].

It remains to be observed that, although I have distinguished between the ideas of a 'general' and a 'particular' Providence, as different aspects of the Divine Government of the world, which have been perceived by different minds, and upon which it may be well for us at different times to dwell, no such distinction can exist for God Himself. It has been well said that "the general providence of God, properly understood, reaches to the most particular and minute objects and events; and the particular providence of God becomes general by its embracing every particular[2]." Even we, in spite of the limitations of our

---

[1] In the Sermon of J. H. Newman's from which I have above quoted a few words, the distinction between the doctrine of a particular Providence and both on the one hand that of a general Providence, and on the other the notion of 'special providences' is well and clearly drawn; while he brings home to the mind what the Doctrine of a particular Providence ought practically to mean for us with that reality and intensity of feeling and power of picturing moral situations, conditions of the inner life, and of discriminating between traits of character, and that subtle force and grace of style, which are characteristic of him.

It may be well for me to add that the attitude towards the world, and life in it, shewn in some parts of this sermon seems to me a mistaken one.

[2] McCosh, *The Method of the Divine Government*, p. 181.

human knowledge, when we reflect upon the unity that is observable in the Universe, marking how events are connected, how objects act upon one another and react, how influences are intermingled, can realise that no act and nothing that befalls may be trivial, that all may need to be taken into account in planning and securing the results that are foreordained.

God, in order to allow freedom to His creatures to develop, refrains, as we must believe, from using His power to prevent many things from being done which are no true expression of His own Will. But it belongs to the very idea which we form of God, that as Infinite Intelligence He must at least know all that happens and is done, and also that as Perfect Goodness He can never be indifferent to the effects produced, and is concerned for the true welfare of individuals, and pays that attention to particulars through which the final results that He desires shall be attained. It has been supposed sometimes that the view that Divine Providence is exercised only in a general way is the more philosophical doctrine. But in truth the only doctrine that can be deemed philosophical is one which includes the belief that all particulars are present to the Divine Mind.

II.   *Divine Providence from the point of view of human experience*

We must now go on to ask whether a belief in Divine Providence as I have here described it, namely, the belief that God's care extends to individual lives, and that He consciously ordains or permits all events, is compatible with and is confirmed by human experience. First of all, and especially, is it compatible with the fact that a considerable part of our experience of the world can be summed up in general laws?

(*a*) Now it should be clearly acknowledged that the circumstance that we are required to direct our conduct in accordance with general laws constitutes an important part of our moral education. We are taught thereby obedience and forethought and a modest estimate of ourselves. It would be difficult to speak too strongly of the immense gain that comes to us through this necessity of conforming ourselves to a general order of Nature. We may, also, surely say that it is far worthier of God that He should act uniformly than with an appearance of capriciousness. But we are not precluded, because our probation and discipline are to a large extent carried on through general laws, from believing that we may individually be objects of the deepest interest to the Divine Mind, while we are undergoing this discipline. Let me take an illustration which, though it is a very simple one, is a natural deduction from that name of Father which Our Lord taught us to give to God. Suppose the case of an affectionate, but at the same time a wise, father who has sent his boy to school. He takes the deepest interest in all that he can hear about him; he follows his course with close attention; he feels keenly for all the trials and temptations to which he may be exposed at the hands of his companions. Yet he knows that he would probably do mischief and make his boy's position worse if he sought to interfere in order to protect him, and that at least he would in so doing deprive him of training invaluable for his future life. He decides that he must leave him to fight his own battles, to make his own way. Now we can see that similarly it would be bad for any of us to be treated in a too exceptional manner. So long as pain and anxieties and disappointments and struggles enter largely into the lot of men generally, it would be the truest misfortune for any one of us to be wholly spared them. We should in that case be too much cut off from sympathy with others, and rendered less serviceable.

(*b*) The very generality, then, of laws of Nature is morally of value to us. But it may be well to guard more comprehensively against the tendency, which manifests itself in the thought even of those who are not consistently materialists, and to which we are all more or less liable, to suppose that if a complete physical explanation of an event can be given by bringing it under certain laws, then the whole reason for its happening is known, and that this disposes of the notion that it can have a moral purpose. But this is an unwarrantable inference. Events in the physical world often do plainly in point of fact have moral and spiritual effects, even of great magnitude; and therefore it is not unreasonable to hold that they were designed to have them. This is no doubt what Bacon means when he says that "both causes" (viz. the 'efficient' and the 'final') may be "true and compatible," and when he goes on quaintly to remark that "the wisdom of God is more admirable when

Nature intendeth one thing, and Providence draweth
forth another[1]."

That effects in the moral and spiritual order should
attend upon physical causes and phenomena is analogous to the strange connexion that there is between
body and mind. Now when we have noted the movements passing through the nerves and brain and the
changes in their tissue, which have accompanied, or it
may be preceded, a process of thought, we should, if
we confined our attention to those physical changes,
have a totally inadequate notion of the whole of what
has happened in any case. And in some cases there may
have been some immortal creation of genius, in many
some exercise of a power of penetrating intellectual
perception, or admiration for that which is beautiful
in art; or again some high resolve may have been
taken, or there may have been aspirations after holiness, or subtle and deadly temptations may have been
nobly resisted. So in the action of physical forces
more generally considered in the world at large, the
physical account, or (as we call it) explanation, of them
may be—nay, I think we may confidently say, is—
very far from being a complete account of the whole
system and plan of things in which they have their
place. Just as in the microcosm, as it appears to us,
there are body and spirit—whatever may be the true
philosophical view of this seeming dualism—so we
may think of the macrocosm as a body linked to a
spiritual element.

Moreover—and this is a point to be specially noted
in the present connexion—moral effects are always

[1] *Advancement of Learning*, II, 7 end.

individual. Though the lessons which we have to learn may often be the same as many others have to learn, and are taught by the same means, they have nevertheless to be personally apprehended.

(c) But we must now go on to note that the reign of law which is to be observed in the world leaves room for a multitude of individual instances. In framing every general law there is a process of abstraction; we neglect what is special in a number of phenomena and seize upon what is common. And the generalising process of our logical faculty is often performed unconsciously, and subjects us to illusion. The danger of taking averages is often pointed out, but we constantly succumb to it. We may forget that we are generalising; and so we fix our thoughts upon that which is common to the exclusion of that which is special in cases where the latter also calls for attention. We attribute to the average, or the law, a reality which belongs only to the individual instances. We may get quite wrong impressions as to the real character of human experience and of the principles which govern human life and destiny from taking men too much in the mass.

Let me enforce this by an illustration from Nature. We observe a patch of colour on a distant hill-side, a certain hue of the rocks. If we draw nearer and seek for its cause we find it to consist in a million specimens of some moss or lichen. In the distance they blend into one hue and give a broad feature to the landscape, and yet each specimen is of different size and form, and comprises many diverse tints, and, most important of all, is living its own life. Just so we may look round upon men in the mass and notice the resemblance in all human life, and may therefore fancy that there is no place left where an individual Divine care over them can have been at work, because we know and imagine so little their private histories and the distinctness of their individual lots.

Moreover, reflect for a moment upon the kind of relation in which individuals stand to laws of nature. Their personal characteristics and their histories appear to be to a large extent determined by them; they must obey them or they will suffer for it. Yet laws so combine, or interfere, enter to such different extents, operating for periods of such different lengths, and with such different amounts of strength, have to be made use of by the conscious minds and wills of different men at such different junctures, that within certain limits an indefinitely great variety of distinct circumstances and experiences and destinies is produced.

The doctrine, therefore, of a Particular Providence is not rendered untenable by the uniformity that has been observed in Nature. There are strains of uniformity, but they are consistent with exceedingly wide variety; and the variety suggests that in the constitution of the world single lives, particular events, particular combinations of circumstances, must be full of significance.

(d) But what is the part played by God's action in regard to all this tangled web of our experiences? That to a certain extent He has limited Himself, so as to leave to human beings a certain measure of freedom, appears to be evident both from our own consciousness and because otherwise we should have to attribute

the existence of moral evil to God. Whether He
similarly allows a measure of independence, of spon-
taneity, to the action of living creatures lower than
ourselves in the scale of being we are plainly not in
a position to judge.

But there would be no doctrine of Providence, and
no effective belief in God, if His self-limitation were
more than partial. We must hold that

> There's a Divinity which shapes our ends,
> Rough hew them how we will;

that He exercises a supreme control, and directs and
guides and apportions, so as to secure that in the
course of the world and of human lives, in spite of
departures on one side and another from the straightest
line to the end which He has determined upon, this
end shall finally be attained. But it may be, and may
ever remain, impossible for human thought to obtain
a view in which it can rest with satisfaction as to how
He does this.

At first sight it may seem comparatively simple to
think of the whole course of the world as having been
present from the beginning to the Divine Mind, and
of His having allowed for the effects of each individual
act of men and permitted them just so far as in His
wisdom He chose. But on further reflection there
will appear to be an inconsistency which cannot be
got over between foreknowledge, even Divine foreknowledge, and any genuine power of initiative, any
truly free beginnings, on the part of men. Lotze[1]
observes that we are hereby "at once thrown back on

---

[1] *Outlines of a Philosophy of Religion*, trans. by F. Conybeare,
§ LXIII, p. 119 f.

the position that this knowledge does not itself share in that characteristic of being *in time*, which it perceives in its objects."

Lotze proceeds: "Let us conceive that the entire reality which for us unfolds itself as a succession, is present all at once to the eye of God. Then what is not really future, but only seems future, in the object will be perceived by God not as an uncertainty, but as something real, nor will its character as free be impaired thereby. In brief, a knowledge of what is free is possible, but a foreknowledge of it is inconceivable. Further than this we cannot go, for we cannot construe to ourselves better than this that timeless imagination which is God's; and so we must reckon-in omniscience with those postulates as to which we know not how they can be fulfilled."

In illustration of this idea of God's thought not being "in time" I may quote the lines from Tennyson's *Princess*:

> To your question now,
> Which touches on the workman and his work.
> Let there be light and there was light: 'tis so;
> For was, and is, and will be, are but is;
> And all creation is one act at once,
> The birth of light: but we that are not all,
> As parts can see but parts, now this, now that,
> And live, perforce, from thought to thought, and make
> One act a phantom of succession: thus
> Our weakness somehow shapes the shadow, Time.

An attempt by Prof. Royce to deal with the contradiction between foreknowledge and human freedom in a manner substantially the same as Lotze does is criticised by Prof. James Ward in his *Realm of Ends* (pp. 312–15). It would not be profitable for me, I think, to try to examine the subject here. Very difficult questions of metaphysics are involved.

It must suffice for me now to say that if we hold that we cannot trust this reasoning of Lotze and Royce and others because it deals in ideas to which there is nothing corresponding in our own experience, then we may observe that as human freedom is (as all experience shews) narrowly restricted, the limitation of God's foreknowledge which is involved will only be partial. The restrictions themselves have been foreordained and so also the result to be finally achieved. Whatever He has decreed will take place and was foreknown.

Further, God's *action* is not to be considered as limited by His foreknowledge. We can think of God as following with His regard the actions of men and their consequences, and as correcting and counteracting what is amiss, to this end employing forces of nature and bringing influences to bear upon human wills, on the analogy of what we ourselves do, though of course in a manner infinitely transcending it.

At any rate the belief that God does in some way order and control events with a view to the fulfilment of His holy and righteous purposes would be untenable only if we were compelled to accept the theory that the world is purely a mechanism, that is to say a closed system of mechanical forces existing and operating in entire independence of Mind and Spirit. Some reasons for rejecting this conception of Nature have been slightly touched upon in this lecture. For a systematic and full exposure of the groundless assumptions on

which it is based and the fallacious reasoning by which
it has been supported I may refer you to Prof. Ward's
Naturalism and Agnosticism. The conclusions of that
work are also summarised in his later book *The Realm
of Ends*; and there is a much briefer but clear treatment of the subject to the same effect by Dr Tennant
in an Essay with the title "The Being of God, in the
Light of Physical Science," in the volume of *Cambridge
Theological Essays.*

(*e*) But you may say: The difficulties which you
have dealt with are in the main theoretic. When they
are removed we may still be left without any positive
ground in our experience for belief in Providence.
Does experience, then, we ask, furnish actual support
for the belief?

In seeking for an answer to this question it will be
important that we should have a clear idea of the
directions in which we should look for it. If we
realise that the great purposes for which life has been
given us are our moral and spiritual discipline, and the
function or functions which we may be intended to
discharge in the general scheme of things for the good
of others, then our belief in Providence will be a belief
that in our passage through this earthly life we are
under the guidance and instruction of a Heavenly
Teacher and Friend, Who in addition to His inward
communications to our minds and spirits, appoints
and uses outward events also with a view to this two-
fold end. And the evidence which we shall expect to
find will be signs of adaptation in our circumstances
to those purposes, discipline suited to our particular
moral needs, indications that mark out for us distinct

duties of some sort, correspondences also between outward and inward leading, and specific lessons taught to us, and through us to others, which seem to be needed as a contribution to the sum of human experience.

The conviction that they have been the objects of such guidance and instruction special to themselves, and have been chosen for special uses, may be felt by different human beings with different degrees of strength. It is only possible for each individual to appreciate the grounds for it in his own case from what he alone fully knows. Yet the faith in Providence which may have thus been bred in him may have been first suggested, and may be confirmed by, the express testimony of others, or by beliefs that are more or less prevalent among men. The very sense itself of a distinct vocation, wherever this is felt, as it is so widely by earnest minds, and as it has been often in an eminent degree by men who have played a great part in the church's and the world's history, is evidence for the reality of God's Providence. For that strong impression has been, we may most naturally suppose, produced by experiences it may be of a startling character, or by occurrences not separately remarkable but noteworthy in their combination.

Again, while God's Hand will be seen in sufferings, losses and disappointments as clearly as, and often more so than, in other events, we shall expect to be able to observe in their apportionment some marks of considerateness (as it were), of fitness to particular cases, of care not altogether to overtax human strength, because God "knoweth our frame and remembereth that we are but dust." St Paul in writing to his Corinthian converts appeals to the fact that in their experience there has been this adjustment to what men are capable of resisting in the matter of temptation, and expresses his confidence that it will continue to be so. "There hath no temptation taken you," he says, "but such as man can bear; but God is faithful, who will not suffer you to be tempted above that ye are able; but will with the temptation make also the way of escape that ye may be able to endure it[1]."

For example, cases of conscience are sometimes propounded for discussion which seem insoluble. But practically it is probably found that the way of men is not so hemmed in as to leave them no right choice, which they will be able to make if they have the needful singleness of purpose and courage.

Once more those compensations which may often be observed in human lots, and which make them— I do not say equal—but less unequal than at first sight appears,—those circumstances whereby calamities are often softened in their incidence and even manifestly turned into blessings, may clearly be put to the account of such a characteristic in the government of the world as we have in view. Misfortunes often thus wear a different face as we look back upon them from that which they have at the time. Shakespeare, who

---

[1] I Cor. x. 13 R.V. The words are very significant for St Paul's view of Providence. The expression rendered "but such as man can bear" means indeed literally "save a human one," which is vague, but the sequel seems to shew that the sense in which the Apostle regarded it as human was that in which the revisers have understood it, and in which also the majority of commentators take it.

in not a few instances gives proof of having profoundly observed religious, as well as other, aspects of human life and character, alludes to this form of experience when he represents Miranda as asking her father, on hearing from him for the first time that he had been duke of Milan:

> What foul play had we that we came from thence?
> Or blessed was 't we did?

And makes him reply:

>   Both, both, my girl:
> By foul play, as thou sayst, were we heav'd thence,
> But blessedly holp hither.

In conclusion, however, let us remember that the evidence for a belief in Providence which human experience can supply is limited by our ignorance. We are rendered to a great degree incapable of judging what the meaning and purpose of much that is appointed for us and others may be by our inability to trace out far the consequences of human words and labour and example. A single word spoken, or deed done, at a particular juncture, may through its influence upon some other person, or in other ways, have far-reaching effects, and the discipline of a life-time and all that served to prepare a man for the moment in question may not be disproportionate if they served to bring about that one result.

The waste, also, that there may seem to be in the sacrifice of precious lives, which would have borne rich fruit if they had been prolonged, as we may feel confident owing to the promise already given, may after all not really have been waste owing to the value which the sacrifice derived from that promise, and the manner in which others have for that reason been affected by it.

But further, if we believe in human immortality we cannot suppose that the harvest from life and death on earth is wholly garnered here.

There must, therefore, always be an element of faith in our hold upon the doctrine of Divine Providence.

PRAYER

1. The word 'prayer' is applied to various modes in which the human soul approaches and addresses God. It may be rightly used of any going forth, as it were, of the soul to God. It is most desirable that it should have for all of us this large meaning whereby the different ends for which we may as we are wont to say 'come before,' or 'seek,' God may be brought together, and we may be led to mark their connexions and relations to one another, and may form a conception of prayer as a whole in which they all have a place. It will be well that those who consider themselves to be for some reason precluded from certain kinds of prayer should realise that there may be other kinds which they might still practise; while those whose minds are embarrassed by no such difficulty should see to it that the different kinds are combined as elements in their prayers in due proportion.

Prayer, then, may take the form of worship, the adoring contemplation of the Wisdom, Goodness, Majesty and Beauty of God; or again of communion with God, in which we lay our being open to God that it may be fully interpenetrated by Him, and endeavour to bring our wills into conformity with His Will. But further, in the view of prayer which has been commonly held by the most spiritually minded, a place has been allowed for definite petitions for the satisfaction of needs and fulfilment of desires pertaining even to our earthly life, and in the public prayers of all portions of the Christian Church it has been assumed and is assumed that this is lawful and right; and there is abundantly clear authority for it in the teaching of Our Lord Himself.

It is especially in connexion with such petitions and the question of their efficacy that difficulties arise; and it is with prayer as consisting in petitions for external objects that we shall to a large extent be occupied in this lecture. But we must not suffer the amount of attention given to prayer under this aspect to make us forget the practical importance of prayer under those other even higher aspects.

2. The subject of Prayer, with special reference to its efficacy in the case of objects belonging to the domain of physical law, was much discussed some 45 years ago. Controversy was specially stimulated by a paper entitled "Prayer for the Sick; Hints towards a Serious Attempt to estimate its value," contributed to the *Contemporary Review* for July, 1872, by Prof. Tyndall, in which he communicated a proposal made to him in a letter from a writer, who was afterwards acknowledged to be an eminent physician, that the efficacy of prayer for the sick should be put to an experimental test by calling upon all the faithful to make the recovery of the patients in a particular ward in some hospital the special object of their prayers for a certain period of time. It was not found difficult to shew in reply that there were practical difficulties

which would make it impossible fairly to apply this test. A particular ward could not be isolated in this way. Believers in prayer would refuse to withhold its benefits from other sick for the purpose of an experiment. It would seem to them inhuman to do so. Moreover, there might always be some persons deeply interested for patients in other wards of the same hospital, who would pray for them all the more earnestly on account of the general summons made on behalf of a different set of people. The proposal also implied a mechanical idea of the operation of prayer to which no thoughtful Christian would assent, as though God must be determined in answering petitions by the number of petitioners, or the time, and amount of breath, expended. It ignored the fact that the possibility of prayers being answered has always in Christian teaching been represented as having some relation to moral and spiritual conditions in the persons concerned, and also to the wider purposes of God. And it was obvious that God might have special reasons for declining to submit Himself to such a test, the application of which might well be deemed in the highest degree presumptuous.

But the discussion carried on in the press and in the pulpit extended to the whole question of the efficacy of prayer in relation to physical law. There has not been any special renewal of the controversy since; but there can be no doubt that the same difficulties are felt, and that the same objections would be urged in some quarters still, as found expression then; so that it is not unnecessary to recur to them. At the same time we ought to be in a better position for considering the subject now, in consequence of all the inquiry that has taken place in the interval into the logical and philosophical aspects of scientific discovery.

It will help to clear our minds in dealing with this subject if we notice one or two of the views that were put forward at the time to which I have referred, by way of compromise between the practice of prayer and the scientific spirit.

One line which was taken by some apologists for prayer we must, I am sure, refuse to adopt. Conceding that it might be unreasonable to expect answers to prayer, or at least leaving the question undecided whether it is so or not, they insisted that prayer should be offered for the sake of its reflex action on him who prays. But it seems clear that this reflex effect could not continue to be produced if the mind came consciously to recognise that there was in the process nothing more to be hoped for than this; indeed prayer would cease to be possible; the real object could not be sufficiently masked, or sought in this indirect way. At the same time we need not hesitate to point to the place which prayer has in our moral and spiritual training as a ground for believing that God means us to pray, and does hear and take account of our prayers. That is of course a very different thing from advocating the practice of prayer merely because of its effect upon ourselves.

Another view, propounded by the Rev. W. Knight, afterwards a professor at St Andrews University[1], is more worthy of notice, for it cannot be charged with

[1] *Contemporary Review* for January, 1873.

unreality like the last. I can imagine that it may at first sight appear to many minds to offer a solution of their chief difficulties. It allows the inviolability of physical law, and at the same time leaves a considerable range for petitions for definite objects, even affecting indirectly outward events. He lays down that our requests ought to be strictly confined to objects falling within the mental, moral and spiritual sphere, and that it is wholly inopportune as regards all that belongs to the domain of physical nature. Where, however, results even in the physical world may be brought about through influencing human minds and wills, there he would allow us to pray for them, for the reason that while thought and will are open to suggestion and influence from within they may themselves lead to action which will determine the course of events. One of his examples will serve to make his point quite clear. "We pray," he writes, "for a friend's life that seems endangered. Such prayer can never be an influential element in arresting the course of disease by one iota. But it *may* bring a fresh suggestion to the mind of a physician, or other attendant, to adopt a remedy which by natural means 'turns the tide' of ebbing life and determines the recovery of the patient" (p. 196).

Now our judgment as to what can be suitably asked of God in prayer may well be affected by what we have observed as to the appointed constitution of the world and course of Nature. This is a point upon which I will touch before concluding this lecture. But the distinction between things physical and mental as conceived and stated in the view to which I have alluded appears to be crude and indeed unsound, and involves consequences that would be serious with regard to God's relation to the world and our relation to Him. It proceeds upon a mistaken conception of the freedom of the will, and of the mental life of man. We may not be necessitarians; indeed necessitarianism does not seem to me to be compatible with a well-grounded Christian Theism. But we must at the same time recognise that the freedom of our wills is strictly limited. Men are not free at any moment to choose whatever they please. Individual characteristics which were congenital, habits which they have formed, and circumstances, go far to determine their impulses, their resolves, their actions. They have a certain power of choice, of adopting as their own this or that one among the motives that are presented to them, of resisting influences that are brought to bear upon them; a certain power, too, of altering their own characters, of winning freedom in directions in which they seemed to have none, or next to none, and on the other hand of forming dispositions which will for the future to a great extent rule them. For the most part, however, such changes take place but slowly. Thus there is an element of fixity at any given time in the moral nature of each man, though it is not so permanently unalterable as physical law appears to be.

But further this question of freedom is essentially a moral one. Without this mysterious element in his nature man would not be a moral being at all. But there is no reason to suppose that the purely intellectual life is free, except in so far as it is affected by the moral element that enters when thought is directed to certain subjects, and careful, sustained attention paid to them, while of others we may refuse to think, with the result that certain mental powers and tendencies may be developed. Thought has been said to be free, but that is in another reference, namely, in contrast with the constraint upon the body that may be exercised by human tyranny. Laws of association hold among ideas which are comparable with the sequences between external phenomena. Between the different choices also which men make, and between these and their characters, there are connexions which are more or less binding. And there appears to be interaction—though we cannot understand how it takes place—between man's moral and mental life and his bodily organism and environment.

It is not correct, therefore, to draw a sharp line between things physical and mental as regards their suitability to be made objects of prayer, on the ground merely that law prevails in the one sphere and not in the other, whatever other grounds there may be for making a distinction between them. So far as there is a difference between the two spheres in this respect, it would have to be stated with many qualifications.

Our consideration in the preceding lecture of the method and character of God's Government of the World ought to make it easy for us to see how matters stand with regard to the possibility of answers being granted to prayer. A moment's reflection will shew that answers to prayer are compatible with the reign of Natural Law precisely in the same way and to the same extent as the exercise of a particular Providence is. If God does indeed order events with a view to the moral and spiritual training of individual men, there can be no reason why He should not be able in so doing to take account of the prayers they offer Him. We have seen that such an ordering of events, at least within a wide range of possibilities, may take place without supposing any changes in physical law, any interference with the natural sequences which Science has discovered, or appears likely to discover. Even we ourselves can modify the course of events by our voluntary actions. And to suppose that there is no guidance and control of the world by God would be to limit His sphere of action beyond even that to which our own is limited.

3. But it may be urged that, although there is not in the supposition that God may answer prayer anything inconsistent with our knowledge of Nature or of our own mental constitution, yet it is presumptuous to assume, as belief in the efficacy of prayer does, that the operation of the All-Wise is accommodated to the views of fallible and ignorant men. This objection may spring from a true feeling of reverence, which deserves respect. But that the objection is not a conclusive one will be evident if we consider that God has manifestly allowed the efforts and labours of men —as also their waywardness and sinfulness—to have great influence on the course of events. He has committed the duty of advancing the cause of His kingdom to men, and has made its success or failure during long periods and in different parts of the world depend to a very great extent on the faithfulness and zeal and discretion of individual men. There is no greater presumptuousness or irreverence involved in

the supposition that He allows the prayers of men to have an effect on His own arrangement of events and stimulation of human wills, than that He leaves a place for their labours.

And there is a fitness in the conjunction of the two, prayer and labour, which makes it reasonable to hold that God has ordained both for us. Though in labour we always use in some measure known means and forces of nature in a way that we do not in prayer, yet even in our labours we are often at fault, we have to act on imperfect knowledge, sometimes almost completely in the dark. We need trust and dependence; the spirit of prayer must animate our labour. On the other hand prayer becomes unreal, if we are not striving to do our utmost.

But there is another point of view, also, from which we may observe the fitness of prayer in relation to our human constitution. In the psychologist's analysis of our mental phenomena *desire* holds an important place. Desire plays a great part in our life. Blind desire lies at the core of our impulses. Conscious desire prompts our intelligently directed efforts. Even when our desires do not lead immediately to action, or are acknowledged by ourselves to be but idle wishes, they affect our temper of mind, our tone of feeling, they are both an index to character and also encourage certain tendencies and so mould character. We are for ever desiring this or that, and we are too prone to desire things that are bad for us as well as that which is of true worth, and also selfishly to limit our desires. Now prayer is a means, and though not the only yet the grandest and most effectual means, for purifying and uplifting desire, and rendering it large and generous.

Prayer supplies us with a standard whereby to judge the rightness of our desires, because if prayer is habitual we become accustomed to bringing desires into God's Presence, and so to considering how they will appear to Him. Desire at its best is noble and holy aspiration, which as prayer ascends to God in order to obtain from Him the assurance that ends which we know to be good shall be achieved, and the strength to do our part in striving for them. In submitting other desires to Him for objects with which our earthly happiness is bound up, we learn to chasten them with the thought that it may not be His Will that they should be fulfilled.

Once more, in prayer an opportunity is provided for exercising desire in regard to ends that are non-personal not merely in the sense that they concern the good of others, but as being such as we are not ourselves engaged in labouring for, and are not in a position to promote by our own efforts. And so our interest in all good causes may be widened and kept alive.

Robert Browning, indeed, in a vision of the famous ones of old represents them as saying:

Each of us heard clang God's "Come" and each was coming;
    Soldiers all, to forward face, not sneaks to lag behind!
How of the field's fortune? That concerned our Leader!
Led, we struck our stroke nor cared for doings left or right:
Each as on his sole head, foiler or succeeder,
    Lay the blame or lit the praise: no care for cowards: fight!

"We struck our stroke nor cared for doings left or

right." So it must be at times in the heat of the battle; and it is of primary importance that each man should cherish the sense of the responsibility which rests on him, and him alone, for doing his utmost at his point in the line, whatever may be happening elsewhere. But that is not the whole truth. There can be no doubt that now our soldiers and our allies at different parts of the far-extended battle-front, West and East and South, are anxious to hear what are the fortunes of the struggle everywhere, and are encouraged by the news of the successes of those who are fighting in the same great cause. We indeed hear that it is so. And in like manner in the life-long conflict to be waged against the Kingdom of Darkness, and for the advance of the Kingdom of God in the world, it is inspiring for all who are engaged in it to think of all others who are so, some of them in fields the most remote from their own, and to cherish a sense of fellowship with them. And this sense of fellowship is powerfully quickened by the belief that through prayer we can really help them, and they us, in our joint labour and strife. Without the conviction that prayer is itself a means for realising a common end, and the habit of employing it, our thoughts amid all that makes demands upon them, are likely to become more and more limited to those efforts that we ourselves are directly by our own obligations concerned in.

4. It remains that we should consider one or two questions which are forced upon our attention from different quarters and on different grounds as to the suitability of certain subjects for prayer. I have

already examined a view which I urged was unsatisfactory as to a distinction between things physical on the one hand and mental and moral on the other. But that is a topic which needs broader treatment.

(a) Before, however, I pass to this there is a question which arises directly out of the thought of that fellowship in prayer, of which I just now spoke between all those who in very different ways and under widely different circumstances are "seeking the Kingdom of God and His righteousness." How far does that fellowship extend? Need it be confined to those who are militant here in earth? None, I imagine, who believe in the life after death will find it difficult or unreasonable to suppose that prayer for those who have been known and loved on earth, and for all the great needs of the world, forms one employment of that life. It has always been a cherished Christian conviction that the blessed departed are engaged in this work of intercession. They may not know our changing circumstances. But they know well what the chief things are which should be asked for in our behalf, if they retain the knowledge of the trials and temptations through which they passed on earth, and of their own efforts after good; which we must hold that they do unless we are prepared to regard the time spent on earth and its hardly bought experience as fruitless.

But may we not also pray for them? Owing to the superstitions and practical abuses which in mediæval times became associated with Prayers for the Dead, there was a strong reaction against the practice in those portions of Christendom which felt deeply the effects of the Reformation. But I think that at the present day many in the Church of England and of other communions amongst us, and belonging to divers schools of thought, will agree with me that the reaction went too far, and that prayer for the departed in the form of a simple commendation of their souls to God for all that they most require is both right and valuable.

There has, perhaps, always been a tendency to conceive of physical death as making a greater change in the life of a human being than in reality it may do. The fact of death may impress our imagination too profoundly, because it puts an end to all visible and tangible participation in life upon this earthly stage, and because also of our ignorance of all that lies beyond. We consequently may be too unwilling to apply to that other life any analogies drawn from this life, and in particular to suppose that the discipline, and even the probation, that are characteristics of this life may be continued there under other conditions. The notion that the state of man is finally fixed for good or ill at death has also been insisted on with a view to increasing the sense men have of their responsibility for using aright the spiritual opportunities of the present life. But there should be sufficient ground for realising this without adopting a tenet which seems to have no real basis in the reason of things, and on which Scripture is silent. It is indeed far more reasonable to think that there may open out before souls the possibility of indefinitely great progress in the life to come, even though at their entry upon that life they may start from very small beginnings of moral and spiritual character.

We may also be confident that the objects in which they come to be supremely interested are the same as the highest that any of us learn to cherish here, and that they are employed in the service of God for realising them, to which we also are called.

These considerations seem to justify our praying for them, and to indicate what the general purport of those prayers may be. It is through praying for them, and through the belief that they, too, pray for us, that we may give practical effect to the article in the Apostles' Creed, "I believe in the Communion of Saints," where saints must be interpreted in the sense which the term has in the New Testament, *i.e.* as denoting all the consecrated, all the faithful, into which company we may well hope many will find themselves admitted in that other world, who in this world appeared to be far too unmindful of their heavenly calling, awakened as they will have been by a new vision of spiritual realities.

We thus obtain, it seems to me, a view in harmony with the thought of the Apostle Paul in certain sublime passages in his Epistles[1], of the manner in which the Universal Father of Spirits is redeeming them all through, and uniting them in, Christ, and leading all forward in a movement, in which He calls them to cooperate with Him and with one another, for bringing about the ultimate victory of Righteousness and Holiness.

(*b*) We turn back now to the very different topic of petitions for objects falling within the domain of

[1] See esp. 1 Cor. xv. 24, 25; Rom. viii. 18—23; Eph. i. 9, 10 and Col. i. 20.

physical law. We have already seen that by distinguishing between a mental and a physical sphere, and allowing to prayer only an influence within the former, the difficulties which it is sought thereby to avoid cannot really be avoided. It was necessary to shew that the scientific observation of Nature rightly interpreted does not involve a view so hard to reconcile with Theism as this one, which implies that God has foregone the power of controlling and directing physical forces for the achievement of moral and spiritual results. Moreover, it is of great practical importance that men's liberty should be vindicated, to pray without reproach for those objects which are nearest to their hearts, provided these are innocent, without making fine-drawn distinctions between things external which cannot, and things internal which can, be granted. That may be left to God. Practically those cannot go far wrong who adhere to what one who had some right to speak described as "the sound philosophy, as well as the piety, of the old Christian practice of 'in all things making our requests known' with the overriding, overruling condition, 'Nevertheless not our will but thine be done[1].'"

Our moral and spiritual training is unquestionably carried on to a large extent through events happening in our outward life. The lessons thus taught us are various. Some of them are stern, and painful to learn, though they should be purifying. But the most fundamental truth that we need to make our own with regard to that outer life is that for it, and for all that

[1] The late Duke of Argyll in the *Contemporary Review* for February, 1873.

is included in it, we are dependent upon God as children upon a wise and loving Father. Now it is possible to regard our outer life in this way, and to pray about the things belonging to it, without asking specifically for any of them. We may pray simply that we may have a right temper of mind in respect to them, a thankful and submissive spirit. But it is not thus that most men learn to pray, or begin to acquire such a spirit. They pray that they may have the earthly good for which they long, knowing as they do so that God may not see fit to grant it, but in the belief that God permits them to ask Him, and that He may therefore give it if they ask, though otherwise He would not. And if they reason about the matter, it may well seem to them that the fact of their humbly and dutifully asking may remove an impediment which would have hindered Him from giving.

All this I hold to be true and important. Nevertheless I do believe that progress alike in natural knowledge and in spiritual does tend to affect the character of our petitions in the direction of concentrating them on moral and spiritual objects. If we have any clear indications, as we think, of God's Will, it can hardly be suitable for us to pray for something different, not because it would not be quite possible for Him to order otherwise, but because the method of the Divine Government in a certain class of cases may seem to have been already made known to us. And the indications of this kind which we may find in the course of Nature increase with our wider knowledge of Nature. Again, we learn alike through the study of Nature, and of Human History, and through our own moral and spiritual growth, to take a larger view of the world's plan and one in which our own individual comfort or earthly life seems to be of small significance. Hence we may feel it to be a kind of impertinence to ask for anything of the nature of favours to ourselves. And at the same time the growth of moral and spiritual character will lead us to care supremely for moral and spiritual ends, while the experience of our own mistakes and misdirected wishes as to earthly good will dispose us to leave all that forms part of it more and more simply in the hands of the Infinite Wisdom.

I think there are many sincere believers in prayer whose feeling in regard to the petitions they can offer is that which I have now expressed. But here we shall be met with a demurrer from those who would not merely, as I have tried to do, maintain the right of men to pray for objects connected with their earthly happiness, but who attribute it to want of faith at the present day that even earnest Christians do not more boldly than they are wont to do ask for things of this order, in particular for the recovery of the sick. They point us to the promises in the New Testament as to the results that should be obtained from the prayer of faith. The disciples, we are told, came to Our Lord and asked with regard to a bad case of demoniac possession, "How is it that we could not cast it out?" And He replied, "This kind can come out by nothing save by prayer[1]." And again He said, "Have faith in God. Verily I say unto you, Whosoever shall say unto this mountain, Be thou taken up and cast into

[1] Mk ix. 29.

the sea; and shall not doubt in his heart, but shall believe that what he saith cometh to pass; he shall have it. Therefore I say unto you, All things whatsoever ye pray and ask for, believe that ye have received them, and ye shall have them[1]." It is urged that these promises were not made only to the disciples of the first days, and that if modern Christians do not obtain their fulfilment it is simply from lack of faith on their part. Indeed it is claimed that in many instances of faith-healing they have been fulfilled.

The evidence as to the reality of the cures alleged is not easy to sift, and the religious question of the efficacy of prayer in relation to them is complicated by the consideration of influences that sometimes come into play when there is no appeal to God. This would not I think be a fitting occasion on which to undertake such an inquiry, even if I were qualified for doing so and there were time for it. I must content myself with making one or two remarks more directly suggested by the line of thought in this lecture.

We should certainly not be justified in saying that answers to prayer so far surpassing ordinary experience that most Christians would not have ventured to expect them, and that they would be commonly called miraculous, have not occurred and may not occur. There seems to be nothing unreasonable in supposing that God has treated men differently in different ages, or that He does so now, in the matter of answering prayer according to the state of their knowledge and their characters. The child can ask, and men in the childhood of the world could ask, for much which it

[1] Mk xi. 23, 24.

would be unnatural for those who are more mature to ask for. The Heavenly Father, Who carries on the education of all His children, may grant answers to prayer conformably with what is fitting at the stage at which they severally are.

But the great end which He has in all His relations with men, namely their moral and spiritual training, must never be forgotten. And I do not think it is unnecessary to observe that in connexion with the practice of faith-healing there is some danger that it may be. An interest in wonders merely as such, which is not religious, or altogether wholesome morally, may too easily be encouraged thereby, while the desire for relief from bodily sickness may take too prominent a place among the objects of prayer. The interests of edification by which St Paul sought to regulate the use of the Gift of Tongues should be applied here also.

In considering yesterday the nature of Divine Providence we saw that it must be conceived as directed to the triumph in the world of Righteousness and Love, and in its care of individuals to their moral education, necessarily in these same qualities. And I contended that human experience as a whole, including our experience of physical law, is not only consistent with, but favours, the belief that God does employ the forces of Nature and the actions of men in a manner to further those great ends. In treating of the function of prayer to-day, I have endeavoured to mark out the place Divinely appointed for prayer in relation to that scheme of Divine Providence.

WAR

Indirectly at least this whole course has been on the war. In dealing definitely with the subject, therefore, it may be that I shall largely repeat what has been already said. But repetition is not always unprofitable, for, to quote Wendell Holmes, "What would Socrates have made out of 'Know thyself,' if he had said it only once, instead of going on, as people complained, always saying it?"

From its place in the syllabus, I take the subject allotted to me to be the religious, not the moral aspect of war—in a word, to be God not Germany, Providence not Pacifism.

For true prophetic insight it might appear that war does not raise the problem of God for us more acutely than peace. Much escapes war, but nothing escapes the devouring tooth of time; wealth oppresses as well as arms; children suffer for the sins of their parents and subjects for the sins of their rulers; the most peaceful life is never anything save a continuous struggle against temptation without and weakness within, and uncertainties of events and the encroachment of old age. In so far as war is of man's causing, it might even seem less to involve the agency of God than other calamities. Yet somehow the prophet has seldom spoken except in face of the worst calamities of war, and even Jesus spoke in view of such tribulation as had not been since the world began.

If we consider how we looked upon the question of God in the long years of our prosperity, we shall perhaps understand. Amid pleasant human relations, secure possessions, varied interests, frequent distractions, the world sufficed us, and few felt any great need of redemption from it. Consequently we both affirmed and denied the existence of God with amazing ease. As we accepted the surface meaning of the world, it was easy to say, this is a pretty good world and must have a benevolent Deity behind it, but it was equally easy to say, this world is sufficient in itself, and needs no such hypothesis to complete it. Both the belief and the unbelief depended on the conviction that this was a comfortable sort of place for sensible people; and naturally neither view was of much help when the present distress came upon us. A true faith, however, does not flourish upon ease and opulence, but is a torch which blazes up highest when the storm is strongest.

War demands another kind of faith, and is primarily important for it, because it is a calamity which admits of no such easy solution. While some accustoming of ourselves to frequent sorrow is necessary for the practical business of life, it is the greatest hindrance to any understanding of life's true meaning and ultimate purpose. War being catastrophic rids us for the moment of the illusion of the slow processes of time, and forces us to see that the repetition of evil is not its explanation, but the accentuation of its misery and the evidence of its usurpation. By thus knocking the spectacles of custom off our eyes, war forces us to consider the evil of the world, and to ask ourselves, if we can be content to believe its final meaning the surface one of pleasure and its ultimate purpose the immediate one of worldly possession. And till we have asked these questions, we have not truly raised for ourselves the question of God at all.

Who can fail to ask them at the present moment, in face of the millions of promising lives extinguished or left maimed and broken, the millions of desolate hearts and bereaved homes, the millions of hungry and homeless and terror-stricken? And in that common human agony we need surely draw no distinction of sides.

At the beginning of the war many soldiers returned from it with the simple faith, that, if God had any regard for humanity and any self-respect as Ruler of the world, He must forthwith interfere to stop so insensate a slaughter. But the war goes on till it has become what a French private soldier straight from Verdun called it, "not war but the blotting out of the peoples."

War, for all who have any vision of its calamity, has thus raised for us the old question of redemption from the world; and till that is raised no real religious solution can be hoped for. At all events, except under the stress of that problem, no thought about God that has been of value to men has ever been produced, for the simple reason that nothing else has faced the evils over which faith is to make us conquerors.

Redemption from the world, however, is only a discerning of the true meaning and purpose of the world, and not a mere discovery that the world is evil.

In one sense doubtless the problem must concern another life. If the departed are only "dust and ashes, dead and done with," what is life in these days but "a tale told by an idiot, full of sound and fury, signifying nothing"? Unless life has a significance beyond its present pleasure, it can have no meaning; and unless there is in another state a victory to crown our conflict, it can have no justifying purpose. Yet the hope of a future life, apart from the meaning and purpose of this, is a mere precipice over which we roll the difficulties of this life, and so lose the profit, even as we escape the pain, of toiling at their solution. Though time may only be understood in its setting in eternity, for us, none the less, everything remains a question of time, so that we find no meaning till we can say amid the welter of human affairs, "The Lord God Omnipotent reigneth," and no purpose unless we can somehow see "the goodness of the Lord in the land of the Living." It will not suffice to relegate God to another sphere, "where the wicked cease from troubling and the weary are at rest," but we need to find something in our present experience which enables us to face all its evil in the assurance that this is God's world and we are God's children.

No eternal and infinite meaning and purpose, however, can ever be manifested in time as more than a vision of hope, a dawn which shines for us more clearly as we set our faces toward the light, as prophetic discernment and not as logical demonstration. If life is not a dead document but a living dialogue, always interpreting itself to those who would understand, we may even rightly speak of revelation. By that I do not mean something merely accepted from another, but a growing purpose manifested to others who have lived more nobly in larger and more moving experiences, without whose help we can no more understand our own experience than, without any education, we can use our own minds. If experience is one, and the history of the race the unfolding in any way of a Divine meaning and purpose, it is the isolation, not of reason but of the madhouse, to think we can make most of our own insight by disregarding the insight of other men. The guidance of their understanding, the inspiration of their courage, the reflection of their blessedness, here, as in every sphere of life in which the issues are vast and distant, are our supreme, our necessary succour.

Thus, and not by dead tradition, are we founded upon the Apostles and Prophets, with Jesus Christ as the chief corner-stone. The prophet is the true organ of revelation, and the supreme mark of the prophet is the determination not to blink any of the world's evil, or rest any hope on thoughtlessness or hardness of heart. Facing the world with sympathetic hearts and sensitive consciences, prophetic souls have suffered above all men, yet out of the darkest judgment, especially of sin, they have won the highest view of human destiny. By that victory they have lived courageously and laboured joyously. The darkest judgment of guilt, expressed in the deepest human agony, which is summed up in the cross of Christ, has, in particular, inspired many who never could give their faith any form of words. Nor are we likely in these days to forget how far the daring of insight and courage go beyond the timidities of argument and prudence, or to fail to understand the value for our own endeavour of those who never shrank from evil, yet never doubted the victory of good.

War thus forces us by its sorrows and its destruction to seek in life a deeper meaning than pleasure and a more enduring purpose than possession. But the special form of its disasters also raises special problems which have called out in prophetic souls special answers.

The first problem springs from the cause of the war.

This desolation has not come from the system of nature which we may believe to have some compensation of good for all its evil, so that, though it may press hard on the individual, it may yet be for the general profit, as when the tempest which wrecks the ships, purifies the air. Being directly due to the machinations of evil men, conceivably at least to the insane pride and regardless ambition of one man, who, as a man, is not stronger or wiser, and certainly no better than ourselves, we cannot even find in it the working of a generally beneficent law, but are left in amazement at the kind of government of the world which allows such calamitous might to one wicked human will.

The second is a problem special to war. War is met by war, organised destruction by organised destruction.

We looked forward to a day of larger consideration for the weak, and of more humble devotion of strength and ability to the common weal, and to a larger recognition that we all find our own in all men's good. We dreamt of a good-will extending beyond the bounds of states, to include at least all civilised peoples in a republic of letters, science, art, religion, labour. Suddenly we found our morning vision of the dawn turned to the black and lightning-riven thunder-cloud of brutal violence and national hatreds. Nor may we delude ourselves into thinking that we ourselves are wholly escaping the spirit of evil. Our hardly won ideas of law steadily give way to arbitrary personal will; men are being driven so hard on the military curb, that many will never respond again to the snaffle of ordinary civil order; an extraordinary hardness is infecting our minds, so that we think less of 100,000 men killed in battle with hundreds dying slowly between the trenches, than we used to do of a small railway accident; and finally we are not always managing to preserve even the ancient chivalries of war, but are allowing our enemies to set the standard.

The third problem is one common to all evil. Yet no other evil gives it such vast expression. It is that the innocent suffer with the guilty.

In this particular war, affliction has been meted out freely all round, and the originators of the war have not escaped. Yet they have not suffered, and, in this life at least, they probably never will suffer like the humble laborious people whom they have used for their own purposes; and still less have they suffered like their homeless desolate victims. Thus we have this problem of the innocent suffering with the guilty, for the guilty, more than the guilty, placarded up on the canvas of a continent.

Thus war raises for us, first the issues of sin, regarding which none of us can say we are not guilty. The Kaiser may apply the torch, but if covetousness is the kind of idolatry that leads to the worship of force, which of us has not added to the inflammable material? Second it forces us to consider what the Apostle calls the Tyranny of Darkness, the corporate nature and cumulative power of evil, in respect of which none of us can say, We have no responsibility. We stand between a kingdom of light and a kingdom of darkness, and there is no escaping the call to conflict. Finally, we have the problem of the sufferings of the innocent, in respect of which none of us can say, We will bear no part, for, in the end, in no other way can evil be undone or good made victorious.

In face of these problems the prophets have set up three conceptions, the most adequate expression of which is to be found in the Gospels. They are the Liberty of the Children of God; the Kingdom of God; the Love of God. A full explanation would be a complete system of theology, so I can merely indicate how, in these things, they took the meaning and purpose of life to lie. The essence of it, however, is that all evil is only the misuse of our powers as children of God, in His family, made in His image.

The Liberty of the Children of God means that God needs sons, and not merely slaves. The Kaiser's enormous power for evil is, as all evil is, only the perversion of our equipment for sharing in God's tasks, so that we may all take it as evidence of the immeasurable possibilities of our choice of good or evil, as a commentary on the comparison between the loss of a soul and the gaining of the world.

Unless the purpose of God in the world is thus dependent on our responsibility, so that the meaning of the present life and the significance of a future life are determined by the uses of our freedom, what light is there on the problem of this war, or, for that matter, on any event in history? As the outcome of a mechanical system of natural law, or of a fixed process of the universe, or of a predestined scheme of things, what can the war be except mere horrible slaughter through unescapable insanity? The more religion is invoked, the more irrational the result. Mechanism is necessarily blind, and fixed process necessarily indifferent; but if these things are of God's directing and doing, following His decree as the planets move by gravitation, and not following in any way the responsibility He has committed to His children, what is the world but a magnified circus, where gladiators fight and suffer, with the thumbs around them forever turned down, but where nothing is ever really accomplished which could not be done as well by wooden puppets on a wire? God is a meaningless word and should be named Fate: while the only amazing thing about the idea of Providence is that it should ever have been planted, even as a wild illusion, in any head which was the product of a world so brutally determined. Unless tremendous issues really depend upon human choice; unless responsibility and character are the deepest, weightiest, most abiding realities; unless the very meaning of our experience is our training to greater freedom by the use, and even by the misuse of such freedom as we already have; unless, indeed, God Himself cannot give us character and make us free by mere gift but only by discipline and duty, what is left us, if not sheer blackness of darkness? If, however, it is of supreme consequence to the Father of our spirits to have children who are not safe merely because they have been shielded from error and wrong, but who have won a victory after which they can neither be bribed nor browbeaten by any form of evil, may we not regard even this destructive conflict, not indeed with the assurance of knowing its meaning so as to escape all sense of mystery and pain, but with the assurance that it has a meaning worthy of all its sorrow as well as of all its courage and willing sacrifice? If free moral personalities are the ground of all value in the universe, if the essence of them is the imputation of all our actions which even God cannot lift from our shoulders and leave us persons, and if even He cannot make us free by the fiat of His omnipotence, but only train us to freedom by the exercise of our powers and the issues of our responsibilities, have we not at least some dim vision of a goal, in view of which we may hope some day, not in this life it may be, but in a greater, to be able to speak of the miseries even of this war as a light affliction but for a moment?

The second answer concerns the kind of order which God bases upon this liberty of His children.

If the rule of God is to be measured by the decent smoothness of the result, nothing can at present be said for it, and neither omnipotence nor goodness can enter into the situation. But, if the true order concerns God's children, and must be of His children's will as well as of His own; if it must be won and not compelled; if, however far round man may wander in the ways of error, he cannot be one with God or with His children till he arrive at the goal of seeing eye to eye with them in truth; if, however hard and mistaken the conflict of will, he cannot be in harmony with God and with His children till he learn to stand shoulder to shoulder in love; if truth and love thus accepted are alone the gold and precious stones with which God builds His Kingdom, then, we can dimly discern some use in all conflict, not only if it spring from some deep-rooted and noble fellowship, and be for any just or lofty cause, but we may even discern a necessity for suffering the burning up of the wood and hay and stubble of worldly motive and selfish purpose. Like all other families, God's family must become a true moral fellowship by cherishing the ties of blood and of association, and by maintaining just rule and right discipline; and only by effort and sacrifice can we pass to the life in which both have disappeared into the spirit of freedom. Thus, dimly at least, we can discern why all progress must have blood upon its garment and upon its thigh and how the only final failure is not to strive, and the only way of not finding God's Kingdom is not to seek it.

If, however, we are only free as we accept, of our own insight and consent, God's rule as our own will, only free as we are gladly bound, only have the liberty of God's children as we cheerfully take our place in His family; if we truly belong to the family of God by the very constitution of our soul; if, in short, all our powers are given us for the Kingdom of God, we can discern how the misuse of human freedom will mean not only evil passion and evil habit in the individual life, but a tyranny of evil organisation in the world. Throughout the ages this evil organisation has received various names and been explained by various theories, both theological and anthropological. Jesus speaks of being delivered, not from evils but from the Evil One—the organised Kingdom of Wickedness; the Apostle Paul speaks of the Tyranny of Darkness and wrestling with Principalities and Powers; Theology has spoken of Original Sin; Science of Heredity and Environment. It means that the powers of habit, association, organisation, cooperation, given us for the Kingdom of God, can be perverted to serve wrong social as well as personal ends, and that progress is only through arraying against each other the forces of right and wrong. The ages we look back upon as the great periods of the world's history have not been times when the large masses of men lived quietly by accepted faiths and customary morals, but when these broke down, often with vast evils to society and apparently with loss to the thoughtless masses of mankind. These losses, however, were compensated for by those who, of their own personal faith and moral insight, heard the imperative call to decision and conflict Such periods of stress are apparently designed, not only for burning up the old social wrongs and worthless safeguards, but for teaching us the weakness of mere parasitic faith and morals and for summoning men with trumpet blast to a new fight of faith, a new warfare of the spirit.

Perhaps the most hopeless thing in our present outlook is our failure to hear that call, our determination to build again our old selfish, competitive social order, with its vast wealth and its measureless poverty, its worthless and restless ambitions, its lack of idealism in service and of brotherhood in fellowship, and to do it by the mere worldly resolve which says "The bricks have fallen, but we will build again with hewn stones." As long as that continues, for all that the nations have suffered, "God's anger is not turned away, but His hand is stretched out still." By that attitude it is plain that we are all involved. Even the Kaiser could only set fire to inflammable material, and if the prophet is right in saying that to use our strength to crush the weak is the same in principle as when the king of Assyria uses his army to annex a country, none of us can say we have lived for such an idea of justice as gives us at this moment a right to wash our hands of all responsibility for the kingdom and power of darkness.

The final answer concerns God's way of establishing His own rule.

If the very essence of God's rule is that it cannot be established by might, even though it be omnipotent might, how does He establish it? He does what the father of the Prodigal did. When he recognised that the lad's purpose was fixed, without argument, he gave him his heritage and let him go. All the time of his son's riot and ruin he did nothing except suffer. But, when the young man came to himself, he was there with every gift that could make forgiveness a reality, there waiting to help him to redeem the past

and secure the future. That vicarious suffering of
the good is what we mean by atonement, and atonement in that sense is the true meaning of saying that
God is love. To be perfect as our Father in Heaven
is perfect, is not to engage in many pious services,
or to do no manner of visible evil, or even to be
supremely good people, but is to love our enemies,
even as God sends His rain upon the just and upon
the unjust.

Such love may require the repression of crime, the
resistance of oppression, the standing in the breach to
protect the weak and the guiltless. Yet when we ask
where the final triumph over evil lies, it is not, it never
is, with "reeking tube or iron shard," but, even in war,
with the readiness to suffer, with the pain and the
sacrifice; and finally it never can be in war at all, but
in the spirit of victorious service which alone can
replace all need for arms. After the thunder, God
is in the still small voice. The final victorious service
is in shouldering the follies and sins of mankind, even
as we would shoulder the disgrace as well as the
sorrow of the brother of our blood. The man who
thinks we can have final peace merely by slaughtering
Germans or by making commercial treaties, and who
sees no need of knitting up again, and more closely
than ever, the brotherhood of man, as the healing
power after this rude surgery, I do not know what he
may be, but he is not of the spirit of Christ, and he
has never understood how Christ's cross is the world's
true meaning, which is not pleasure and profit, but
discipline and duty, and he has no vision of the goal
of the world which is to be the Kingdom of God

established in the liberty of His children, through the service and sacrifice of love.

When we raise the question of God, we are raising the question of the meaning and purpose of life. In the end it is the question of our own personal moral values against the might of violence and brute force. The externality of our arguments and the formality of our religion have often separated the belief in God from everything for which the name of God stands. Too often we have left the impression that we might believe in none of the things Christ lived for and yet be good Christians, or, on the contrary, take up His attitude to life every day in trust in the powers of righteousness He believed in, and yet not be Christians at all. For example, a discussion arose among some soldiers on the needs of the country. A regular, a man of modest attainments but of marked ability and fine spirit, maintained that, above our need of a great statesman or even a great general, was our need of a spiritual leader. Though I have never heard finer or better expressed Christianity, and though he knew that he was echoing the Gospels, he prefaced each departure of his argument with the phrase, "Though I am not a Christian." By contrast I was reminded of the saying attributed to a certain bishop: "In my diocese there is not a single person who ever thinks a Christian thought or utters a Christian sentiment." Yet I suppose many there called themselves Christians.

We must rid ourselves of the idea that we can believe in the might of goodness and not in God; and in God and not in the might of goodness. When we are reasoning about God we are considering whether, in spite of the success of wickedness, wickedness wins the final success; whether, in spite of the power of violence, violence is the final power; whether the meaning of the world is cruelty and cunning or truth and goodness. The question of God is precisely the question of the meaning and purpose of the world, and that resolves itself into the question whether truth is the last reality and goodness the one imperishable possession.

COMPETITION BETWEEN INDIVIDUALS AND CLASSES, CONSIDERED FROM THE CHRISTIAN POINT OF VIEW

Such is the subject assigned to me. I propose to deal with it by considering Competition as we see it in the world in which we live. Then I shall sketch the Christian ideal of social order, and lastly consider what possibilities there are of human society passing from the present competitive organisation to one more in accordance with the Christian ideal.

When I speak of Competition I mean the desire of acquisition, of possession, and the rivalry which results when individuals and classes strive to extend their claim to the ownership of things. This differs from healthy emulation in which the main desire is to do something well, and in which the pleasure results from the performance; the pleasure of the scholar, of the skilled workman, of the artist, of the man of science. Competition played very little part in the life-work of our great scientist Darwin. He did not write the *Origin of Species* in order that he might get money, though his publisher gave him a cheque for his MS. There may be rivalry, jealousy and uncharitableness among men of science and artists, and if report speak true there often is, but it is a rivalry in performance, in reputation, but not in acquisition.

Rivalry in acquisition begins in the nursery. The little girl grasps a toy and says, " This is mine." Her youthful brother says, " No, it is mine," and endeavours by force to secure possession. The wise parent says, " Neither of you shall have it unless you share it."

Unfortunately in later life we are not compelled to share, and the desire to acquire things and call them mine tends to become the ruling passion, and as the things which men desire to call mine are limited, rivalry of desire results in fierce competition for possession. Undoubtedly the desire of acquisition is a powerful stimulus to exertion. Some say it is the only one which will effectively operate permanently, day in and day out. Other motives may work under special excitement, but self-interest and especially in the acquisition of things is the permanent stimulus in this work-a-day world, and therefore competition is as much a law of nature in the moral order, as gravitation in the physical.

Undoubtedly the freedom to acquire, which was the essence of the *laissez faire*, or ' let alone ' policy of the last century, did result in an enormous increase of wealth. Under the stimulus of self-interest, each man working for himself did raise productive power to a high degree of efficiency. The possessions of the individuals composing the nation increased enormously, and the total income grew with leaps and bounds till before the war it was estimated at £2200 millions per annum. But notwithstanding that, the majority of the population had few possessions—*e.g.* in London, the richest city in the world, Mr Chas. Booth, as the result of careful investigation, estimated that 30 % of

the population of London were on or below the poverty
line; *i.e.* that their earnings did not exceed 21s. a
week per family. Mr Seebohm Rowntree's examination of the conditions of life in the provincial and
Cathedral City of York yielded very similar results,
i.e. about 30 % on or below the poverty line, and he
estimated that 15 % of the working classes were in
primary poverty, had less than sufficient to provide
the minimum of food, clothing and shelter.

Competition creates a state of war in which each is
fighting for his own hand, for the acquisition of wealth.
Rival traders may preserve the forms of friendship, but
they are impelled to hostile acts, each seeking to go
one better than his rival, to out-general or out-advertise
him.

We know how a business with an unscrupulous
head—a good man of business!! will crush the smaller
men in the same trade ruthlessly, will defraud the
public where it can be safely done, will water capital,
float companies of more than doubtful soundness, and
will, if he can, reduce wages and sweat labour because by
so doing he can gain more, or thinks he can. Granting
all the energy and the organisation which Competition
calls forth, the moral history of ' big business ' makes
sorry reading. The cause is that Competition puts men
in the relation of antagonism and not in the relation
of friendly cooperation. It is war, and the wonder is,
not that it drives men to harsh and fraudulent action
to secure success, but that so many act honestly and
treat others with as much consideration as they do.
Wage economic war in the spirit of sportsmen, and not
in the spirit of Germans.

The popular doctrine of the early Victorian era that the well-being of the community would be best secured by every man looking after his own interest has proved a delusion, for free competition gives an advantage to the strong, and the strength to acquire increases in geometrical progression, a fact which we recognise in such proverbs as 'nothing succeeds like success,' 'money breeds money.' It is those who possess wealth, or control wealth, who can seize new sources of wealth, or as we say find new outlets for their capital. When a new seam of mineral, or a new process is discovered, it is not the poor man but the financial magnate who gets hold of it, and uses his hold of it to increase his possessions.

Competition which gives such an advantage to the strong does not limit the advantage to the strong morally, but tends to confer advantage on the unscrupulous. There are those who contend that no man can succeed in competitive business and remain honest. That is an exaggeration, but it is not far from the truth. Competitive industry and the advantage it confers on those who already have over the 'have nots' was never more admirably described than by that inimitable creation of the genius of Dickens, Samuel Weller, in the words "Every man for himself and God for us all, as the elephant said when he danced among the chickens." A very comforting view of providence for the elephant, but one likely to make the chickens blaspheme when they are told it is the arrangement of a beneficent providence.

The more wealth, especially that which is strictly limited in quantity like land, passes into the hands of the few, the less is left for the rest. As private possession increases, common wealth decreases. If a man "lay field to field till he dwell alone in the midst of the earth," the fewer fields there are for the rest of the community.

Under the system of competition the larger part of the wealth is in the possession of the few. Far as this process has proceeded in England it has proceeded still further in America where competition has been allowed more unrestricted sway. A comparatively few men own, or control, the vast natural resources of that vast territory, and it has become a serious problem how the natural resources of America shall be regained for Americans.

Among the evil results of competition may be briefly enumerated the following: The raising of the desire of possession as the ruling motive tends to moral debasement, and to the measurement of worth by material possessions. Those who have, become a class apart, who look down on those who have not, and thus the inequality which results from competition undermines the sense of brotherhood. The pedestrian finds it difficult to look upon the man who covers him with the dust of his Rolls-Royce motor as a man and a brother. And the man in the Rolls-Royce, lolling in comfort, is apt to regard the begrimed pedestrian as an inferior being.

The inequalities of wealth result in extravagant luxury of the relatively few, who possess far more than they can profitably use, and in the poverty of the many who lack the essentials of life, and who are by the exigencies of their poverty deprived of the chance of the development of the higher faculties. Moreover, luxury with its manifold forms of self-indulgence undermines the character of the rich much as over-eating ruins the health of the body.

Then again competition, in spite of the energy it evokes, is extremely wasteful, for it hinders wise organisation of effort. There are half a dozen milk-sellers in one street where one would suffice. There are rival commercial travellers, rival advertisements. The main reason of the tendency to combination in business is the enormous economy which results from the reduction, if not the elimination, of competition. That the elimination of competition should be economical proves the waste of competition. I might enumerate many other evils did time permit, but the greatest of all is perhaps the way in which the concentration of thought and energy on getting wealth leads to the neglect of human welfare and tends to make profits and dividends rank before the health and well-being of the persons engaged in the industry; as witness the long list of factory legislation found necessary to protect the worker from exploitation and secure a minimum of protection. It is true that this policy of exploitation is foolish as well as wicked, for insanitary conditions, long hours of work and lack of interest in work destroy the efficiency of the worker, and in the long run reduce output and therefore profit. Read the report issued by Sir George Newman on the result of overwork in munition factories, the effect of Sunday labour, long hours and absence of facilities of obtaining good food. Also note what the Government reports say of the economical advantages which result from the employment of welfare workers.

We have seen with our own eyes the wonderful physical improvement in the factory hands and agricultural labourers who have entered the army, in consequence of their being well fed and clothed, and living in fresh air instead of in slums and insanitary cottages. But the immediate money interests of the employers or shareholders seem to be opposed to expenditure on the welfare of the employee, or to giving increased wages to promote physical efficiency. Selfishness is invariably short-sighted, it does not take long views, and the result is wasteful; as when for the sake of immediate profit it denudes a countryside of trees, or works only the thickest seams of coal; wasteful of human material from decreased efficiency and loss of willing cooperation.

I remember when I visited some works where very large sums were expended on promoting the welfare of the employees I said to the Managing Director: "I have no doubt all you have shown me has been done from the best and most unselfish motives, but I believe it pays." "Yes," he replied, "that is what we contend. There is no expenditure which is so remunerative as that we have incurred to secure the welfare and happiness of the employees."

Let us now turn from individualistic competition to class competition which is its necessary corollary; for when competition has concentrated wealth in the hands of the few the disinherited are compelled to combine to resist the pressure which those who hold the means of life can bring on those who have not. Hence we have Capital and Labour instead of being hearty co-operators in their common work divided into hostile bodies, each striving to obtain a larger share of the wealth produced—the employer to pay as little as he can, held in check by the fear of a strike; labour demanding as much as it dare, the demands held in check only by fear of the suffering which a strike or lock-out will entail. In this struggle the combinations grow ever larger and larger, Employers' Associations unite, Trade Union combines with Trade Union, till the time comes when the whole of those who have are arrayed against all those who have not, and then you have the Class War. We were dangerously near such a War when the war between nations broke out two years ago. This condition of things is not peculiar to England. It exists in every country in which the competitive system prevails, it is the necessary inevitable outcome of a society organised on the principle of competition, of the idolatry of covetousness as St Paul calls it, the putting up and worshipping as the deity governing human action the false deity of covetousness, or the desire of possession. If I have passed over without mention the many efforts made in many directions to check and limit competition it is not because I am not aware of them, but the broad features remain; wealth infinitely greater than any community has ever possessed concentrated in the hands of the minority, many of whom become demoralised by luxury, and on the other hand a vast multitude ill-fed, ill-clothed, ill-housed, condemned to live narrow mean lives with little if any opportunity of developing the higher faculties; and a rankling sense of the injustice of it all leading up to an antagonism between those who have not and those that have, which may end in War—a war which would be more destructive than even the awful war now raging in France, Belgium and Poland.

Now let me turn from the world as it is to the Social ideals of the Gospel. That ideal is essentially that of the family. Its basis is the recognition of the brotherhood of men because all are children of the one Father, all are akin to Him, because they have a spark of the divine in them, and all as His children are equally precious in the sight of God, equally entitled to the full opportunities of life. The only effective basis for the idea of the Brotherhood of man is belief in the Fatherhood of God. It was the Christian doctrine of the brotherhood of man which was the basis of the agitation for abolition of negro slavery. The negro had a soul, was a son of God and therefore a man and a brother.

It is this which makes those who preach belief in the superman, and who consider themselves supermen, such bitter opponents of Christianity. In an ideal family the ruling principle is not competition but mutual help. It is not considered fair that the family arrangements should confer greater advantages on some members rather than others. It is not a dead level, for one may be cleverer than another, one may be industrious, another lazy, and therefore their success may vary, but the clever will help the stupid, the industrious try to cure the lazy.

If we turn to the words of Christ as handed down to us by St Luke in the 22nd chapter, we find Christ's condemnation of competition as the motive of action, and the motive He desires should be substituted for it.

Let me read the passage: "There was a strife among the disciples as to which of them should be accounted greatest." (The spirit of competition, the desire to acquire honour for themselves was strong.) "And He said unto them, The kings of the Gentiles exercise lordship over them; and they that exercise authority upon them are called benefactors." In other words this spirit of competition was a heathen ideal. Then He added, "But ye shall not be so; but he that is greatest among you, let him be as the younger; and he that is chief, as he that doth serve. For whether is greater, he that sitteth at meat, or he that serveth? Is not he that sitteth at meat? *but* I am among you as He that serveth."

Thus Jesus substitutes service instead of competition as the motive of action. The object of effort not self-aggrandisement, not making one's pile, but serving the community. What an England it would be if all the ability, all the energy, all the best thought of Englishmen were devoted to promoting the welfare of the community, and if the chief rivalry among us was the rivalry of service!

Life would be better and infinitely happier because the spirit would find higher expression and work being unselfish would be a joy. The war has brought great sorrow, but I believe there are many who have been happier since the war than they ever were before, for they have been living a life of unselfish service; and this is especially true of women, for the war has opened up to them so many avenues of service which did not exist before. "Oh," said a society lady who was working amid the wounded in France, "Oh, I don't know how I ever lived my old life of frivolity and amusement. I would not go back to it for anything." Try to picture an England in which the sense of brotherhood was so strong that the welfare of the brotherhood of the community was the dominating concern of all, and in which honour, reputation, success were all measured in terms of service.

Then contrast that picture with the competitive England in which we live, to some features of which I have alluded. There can be no doubt as to which would be best to live in, and that true wisdom and the true principles of social organisation are to be found in the social ideals of Christ.

A friend of mine who has given literary expression to some of the most Christian utterances that have appeared during the war said to me in course of conversation, "I used not to be a Christian, and I was not what is commonly called converted, but I came to believe in Christ because when I thought things out I realised that Christianity is the only thing which will work in this world of ours." He was right—Christianity is the most practical thing in the world.

Perhaps you think however attractive the Christian social ideal may appear it is a social ideal for angels but not for men. Yes; but the Christian contention is that man has the capacity of becoming an angel because he has the spark of the divine in him, and the power of evoking the help of the Spirit of God.

The Christian ideal is the practical ideal, is the only ideal which will work. *E.g.* all are agreed in thinking that the present industrial system fails to reconcile the interests of Capital and Labour and that because the wage-earner has no direct concern in the prosperity of the business in which he is engaged, no say in the management of the industry in which he is employed, he loses interest or pride in his work, has no stimulus to do his best, and that this is demoralising to his character and lessens his efficiency. How to alter this and so change the position of the wage-earner that he may realise that his interest and the welfare of the business in which he is employed are identical is the problem which the best minds and best hearts are endeavouring to solve by experiments in cooperation, profit-sharing and so on. But above all one longs for the day when representatives of the workmen shall sit on the Board of Directors and thus enable the wage-earners to realise the solidarity of the interests of Capital and Labour, that they are in reality partners in the business in which they earn their living. Labour has passed from slavery to serfdom, from serfdom to that of hireling, and the day is dawning when the transition from the position of hireling to that of partner will take place. Sir George Livesey pointed out the way in his work with the S. Metropolitan Gas Co. That principle with necessary adaptations to the circumstances of the various trades may well be copied. In other words we have come to realise that what industry needs is the application of the Christian ideal of mutual cooperation for a common end.

Now let me pass to the third section of my subject, viz. to the possibility of mankind passing from the present competitive social organisation to a Christian social organisation based on brotherhood and service.

Here it is worth noting that all real progress

has consisted in approximation to the Christian ideal.

The idea which is at the root of all our factory legislation is a family idea. The community steps in, and in the interest of the family of the nation limits competition, limits the power of those who possess the means of life to oppress the weaker members of the family by taking advantage of their necessities.

National education is a recognition that every member of the family should have opportunities of developing his mental faculties. It is a very imperfect recognition of that principle, for it does not give equal opportunities to all. Broadly speaking it is elementary education only for the 'have nots,' and higher education for the children of the 'haves'; and in war time when labour is needed for agriculture farmers who agitate for the reduction in the leaving age to 11 years see no inconsistency in keeping their own sons of 16 or 17 at secondary schools.

Still, apart from this reaction caused by the war, the effort of the community has been for years in the direction of more equal educational opportunities for all—an approximation to the Christian ideal. Again, the extension of the suffrage is really a practical application of the family principle, a recognition that every member of the family has an equal concern in all that affects the welfare of the family. A right independent of property or any other consideration than membership in the society. A right which we have come to recognise as spiritual, as not based on the possession of property but on the possession of a soul, because "a man is a man for a' that." It is true we have only admitted half the family, but the other half cannot be much longer excluded, especially after such a striking exhibition of women's capacity and service to the community as has been given during the war.

But I must not weary you by going through the details; it must suffice ·to remind you of the extent to which the community as a whole has shouldered the burdens of the weak, and made provision for their welfare by Old Age Pensions, Insurance Act, Care of Consumptives, Medical Inspection of School Children, Health Nurses, Maternity Provision, Unemployed Benefit, and so on. There has also been a great extension in public property for the benefit of the community—public parks, free libraries, art galleries and so forth.

In such things as these we have the index figure of real progress and not in the number of Rolls-Royce cars or the quantity of diamonds worn at a Court levee. In other words, the true measure of progress is approximation to the Christian ideal.

Competition, limited by sanitary regulations, still rules in housing, and results in dreary streets depressing to the higher faculties; and in overcrowded slums where the death-rate among the 'have nots' is several times greater than among the suburbs of the 'haves.'

Letchworth and garden suburbs indicate possible improvement, and I would have you note that their success lies in the extent to which they eliminate competition by collective ownership, and are therefore able to make human welfare and not private gain the first consideration in estate and house planning. They succeed because they embody to some extent the brotherly, social, family ideal. Yes. But you cannot carry on trade without competition, it is its very life-blood, and if you did take it away energy would be weakened as is the case when monopoly is created. Those who argue thus may well be reminded that by far the largest trading concern in the United Kingdom is one which works without profit and pays no income-tax. I refer to the Cooperative Society, which grows food, grinds corn, makes clothes and wall-paper, imports tea and sugar and carries on a vast series of industrial activities the annual value of which is £140,000,000.

The spirit of War is fundamentally opposed to the spirit of Christianity, but when it is urged that it is impossible to conceive a social order in which enthusiasm for the common good can be more powerful than self-interest one need only point to our volunteer army in France. They are working hard, suffering hardship, risking life and limb, not for self-interest, but for the community, for England. The reward they covet is the D.S.O., the recognition that they have rendered distinguished service to the country. What the D.S.O. and V.C. are in the army peerages and knighthoods would be in a Christian social organisation; recognition of the value of services rendered to the community. But another of the many lessons the war is teaching us is the possibility of taking the supply of needs out of the operation of competition and the advantage of doing so, as for instance the buying up of sugar, the taking over the railways, organising industry in the production of munitions. If these things can be done for the benefit of the army they can be done for that of the community. May we not also hope that the war may do a great deal towards quickening the sense of brotherhood. All classes have been working together for a common object, have been living together and risking life together. All agree that the 'Tommies' have been splendid, heroes every one; and none have been more struck with the cheerfulness with which they bear pain and their innate gentlemanliness than the nurses in the hospitals. These heroes and gentlemen can no longer be spoken of as the lower order or regarded as wicked and unreasonable men who will go on strike, nor can the nation continue to acquiesce complacently in the slums as suitable dwellings for such men. Conversely the men from the slums, men from the factory and mine have been living and working with those they used to call the idle rich. They find them men like themselves who share the same hardships, and willingly take more than their share of risks, men animated with the same determination, the same hopes. Thus both the 'haves' and the 'have nots' realise a spiritual oneness such as they had not realised before.

Grave industrial problems will face us after the war, the industrial dislocation will be of a magnitude beyond all precedent, but we can never be content to go back to the conditions which prevailed before the war. The hope for the future is that we shall move more and more away from the ideal of competition and towards the realisation of the Christian ideals of Brotherhood, Justice and Service.

Whether that transformation will take place and the rate at which it will proceed will depend on the extent to which Christians really believe in the teaching of Christ, and the strenuousness of their efforts to convince men of the wisdom of that teaching.

COMPETITION BETWEEN NATIONS, CONSIDERED FROM THE CHRISTIAN POINT OF VIEW

This is a natural sequel to the consideration of Competition between individuals and classes which occupied us in the previous lecture. Competition between nations merely carries into the international sphere the ideas which play such a large part in our daily life, and the habits of our economic activities.

Nations like individuals measure greatness by the extent of possessions, and exhibit the same desire of acquisition and aggrandisement; and consequently there is the same clashing of rival interests, and the same tendency to secure material gain with scant regard of moral considerations, and with an even more cynical will to power for its own sake and as a means whereby wealth may be acquired.

This desire of possession expresses itself partly in an endeavour to acquire more of the surface of the earth, partly in obtaining economic advantages.

In the main such competition is a competition of might in which right becomes a secondary consideration, if not entirely negligible. Let me give a few examples. I will not go back to the scandal of the partition of Poland, but confine myself to instances of territorial acquisitions effected in my own lifetime.

In 1864 Prussia deliberately went to war with Denmark because Denmark was weak and her allies, England included, were unwilling to fight, and wrested from her the provinces of Schleswig and Holstein. Norman Angell says that it is an illusion to imagine the conquerors really gain by such annexation, as the houses and lands remain in the possession of the people of the country annexed, and that no German outside a few officials who got jobs was a penny the richer. Norman Angell is right up to a certain point, but every Prussian had the sentimental, but none the less real satisfaction of seeing a larger area of the map painted in the Prussian colours, and that ministered to his desire of possession. Moreover such conquest often removes a tariff barrier and may open up trade facilities; but what is perhaps most important of all in national competition, by adding population it increases the number of soldiers and enables the governing power to impose its will more effectively.

By the war of 1870, brought about by the deliberate falsification of a telegram, Germany added to her territory Alsace and Lorraine. In so doing her rulers were actuated solely by what they believed to be her interests. The justice of their action never entered into their consideration. Might was on their side and right did not matter.

In 1885 the great European powers partitioned the whole continent of Africa between them. I see Mr Lowes Dickinson describes this partition "as one of the wisest and most far-seeing achievements of European policy." If it was, it was because it checked competition for a time by leaving no claim unstaked;

but scant consideration was given to the claims of justice even among European states. Of course black races do not count! Sweden, Norway, Holland being small, and possessing insignificant military force, had no part or lot in the division. Belgium, it is true, obtained the Congo, but that was due to the astuteness of the infamous Leopold who played upon the jealousies of England and Germany, and convinced them of the advantage of placing the rich basin of the Congo under the control of a weak power, and a philanthropic monarch.

When Russia was weakened by her war with Japan, and not in a condition to fight, Austria annexed Bosnia and Herzegovina, contrary to the terms of the treaty of Berlin, and retained them because, as she had rightly calculated, no one thought it worth while to go to war to prevent her.

France annexed Tunis, Algeria and Morocco in spite of promising at the Congress of Algeciras she would do nothing of the kind.

Italy, when Turkey was weakened by the Balkan wars, seized Tripoli because she had the power to do so.

But the rival interests of nations come even more into collision in the economic sphere, in the desire to secure products which are essential to industry. We divided Persia into English and Russian spheres of influence because of our interest in the Persian Gulf; and it was the need of making our oil supply safe which was the original reason for sending a British force into Mesopotamia. Germany's need of raw material for her industries impelled her to seek influence in Turkey which would enable her capitalists to develop the rich

sources of Asia Minor and hence the German struggle
to secure control of the railway to Bagdad.

Then there are the struggles of groups of financiers
to obtain concessions of all kinds, to make loans and
so gain control, make waterworks, work mines, build
railroads and so on; and these seek for, and more or
less receive, the support of their respective governments. I have mentioned these well-known facts
because I want to make it clear that international
relations are a vast network of competition which is
waged all over the world; and as competition tends
to lower the moral standard in business at home, so
it does even more lower international morality. The
morals of international politics are the morals of
Macchiavelli, from the unblushing trickery of Bismarck and his cynical appeal to blood and iron, to the
trickery and unscrupulousness of the great groups of
financiers.

Everything is said to be fair in love and war, and
certainly a study of international politics will convince
one that diplomacy has very often acted on that motto.

If you doubt it read Bismarck's *Memoirs, European
Anarchy* by Lowes Dickinson, *Ten Years' Secret
Diplomacy* by E. D. Morel; or a very remarkable
book by Arthur Bullard, an American, entitled *The
Diplomacy of the Great War*—from which I will quote
the following passage: "We cannot reasonably expect
diplomats to observe a higher standard of morality
than members of Parliament and business men. Competition is still the rule of life in the internal affairs
of christendom. Mutual aid is as yet only a pious
ideal. In industry everywhere we see this bitter

spirit of conflict. One group of oil interests—to take one example—and it is just the same with the trade in milk or clothing—tries by hook or crook to get an advantage over its rivals, to gain supremacy in its particular world. We see manufacturers uniting in powerful fighting ententes to resist in common the aspirations of their employees. We see working men everywhere combining in offensive and defensive alliances to fight for their rights. With such rivalry and bitter conflict between neighbours it is hardly surprising that there has been little which could be called 'peace' in the relations between nations."

Between the nations there is keen competition for both dominance and possession, and it brings forth its natural fruit of ill-will, unscrupulousness, disregard of morality, and is only held in check by war, or fear of war.

As long as we base our civilisation and our habits of thought on the idea of competition between individuals there will be competition between the groups of individuals which form nations. As long as we allow the competition within the nation to work out the manifold injustices which are the commonplaces of our daily life there will be injustices between nations. The War though primarily caused by Germany is to a great extent the product of the evil spirit of our time, its natural, if not its necessary outcome.

I venture to think that the greatest danger and the one most likely to imperil a stable peace is the idea which finds favour in many quarters, that Germany shall be punished after the war by imposing on her trade disabilities. It may be necessary to take measures to prevent Germans controlling commercial companies in the Allied countries, or obtaining financial control of their industries because such opportunities have been abused in the past, but do not let us keep an open sore by endeavouring to penalise German trade. If we persist in a trade war, not a trade rivalry, but an organised war, to penalise Germany there can be no permanent peace—the peace after the war will be merely a suspension of military hostilities, a temporary armistice, not a real peace.

Now let us turn from the world dominated by Competition, with its greed of possession, its policy of grab, its belief in force, and its consequent perpetual conflict of interests which keeps the nations in a continual state of mutual fear, and on the brink of war, to the Christian ideal of international relationships.

For the will to power the Christian ideal substitutes the will to justice. "Seek ye first the Kingdom of God and His righteousness." Each nation willing to subordinate its own interests to the claims of justice, and neither seek nor desire to obtain any unfair advantage over its neighbours. The transition from the will to power to the will to justice will be long and difficult of accomplishment, for it involves belief in honesty of purpose on both sides, a genuine acceptance of the principle embodied in Penn's celebrated treaty with the Indians, "that neither party will lightly believe evil of the other."

Creighton in his *History of the Papacy* gives an interesting account of how Æneas Silvius when he had attained to the Papacy turned virtuous, but as he had in his earlier career as a diplomatist tricked every statesman in Europe no one would believe in his honesty when he really was honest, and therefore all his schemes for a European confederation against the Mahommedans failed miserably. It will not be easy to convince Englishmen of the diplomatic honesty of Germans, or Germans of the diplomatic honesty of Englishmen, even when they are honest.

As for the will to power the Christian ideal substitutes the will to justice, so for the rivalry and greed of competition it substitutes goodwill, friendship and the honest desire of the welfare of each; and it is worthy of note that in the modern rendering of the song of Bethlehem peace is only promised to men of goodwill. "Peace on earth to men of goodwill." But the chief obstacle on earth to goodwill is the desire of possession, and the idea that greatness is measured by the extent of possession, by territory and wealth. Christ's estimate of values is entirely different and He teaches us that a man's life consisteth not in the things he possesseth, and that the greatness of a nation no more than that of an individual consists in possession; that greatness is greatness in life, in character, in spiritual achievement, in soul. That true greatness lies in spiritual achievement rather than in material prosperity was admirably expressed in Cardinal Mercier's brave and eloquent pastoral, in which after describing the sufferings his flock had endured and the losses they had sustained, he exclaimed: "Is there a patriot among us who does not know that Belgium has grown great? Which of us does not exult in the brightness of the glory of this shattered nation?"

The history of the world endorses the verdict of

Jesus. The two greatest nations the world has ever known were two small nations. The Jews, and the Greeks before the conquests of Alexander of Macedon. It is they who have left the deepest mark on the world, conferred the greatest service on mankind. To the one we owe our highest spiritual ideas; to the other philosophy and the most glorious achievements in Art. They have indeed been the world's schoolmasters, and to this day our school curriculum is based on the religious ideas of the Jews and the intellectual conceptions of the Greeks. Whereas the successive empires of Assyria, Babylon and Persia, which were great in territory, great in possessions, great in military force, have left to the world little permanent evidence of greatness beyond neglected and sand-covered ruins.

It will not be out of place to remind ourselves that the true greatness of England does not consist in the extent of her far-flung empire on which, as we say, the sun never sets, but that among the small people of this small island there was wrought out by the circumstances of our history the methods of representative government, which made government of the people, by the people, for the people possible. The glory of England is that she rendered other nations the service of teaching them the lessons she had learnt, and thus became the mother of Parliaments. The glory of England in the future will not be measured by the area over which she has held sway in India and Egypt, but by the degree in which she succeeds in teaching the peoples in those countries to govern themselves, and raises them to a position like that of the self-governing colonies of Canada and Australia, able to dispense with any exercise of power by us, free self-governing communities united to England by bonds of sympathy and friendship.

We may sum up the Christian ideal of international relations somewhat in this fashion.

The nations are groups of the great family of God's children having equal rights, living in friendship, no nation desiring to dominate over others, or acquire the possessions of another, regulating their relations by justice, neither seeking nor desiring more than the law allows; each developing its own resources, its own capacities, its own character and spiritual gifts, and by friendly interchange contributing to the welfare of the whole human race. That is the Christian ideal, a world without the lust of power and possession, without greed and competition, a world of international service, a world of goodwill and of peace.

There can be little doubt that if instead of worshipping the false god, the idol of covetousness, which is the root of the will to power and will to possess, and which exalts competition as the law of life, men accepted the Christian ideal, the world would be infinitely better and happier: and that the Christian ideal so far from being unpractical, and one that will not work, is the only ideal which will bring peace and happiness to men.

But it is an ideal which is sadly far from realisation, so far as to seem entirely and hopelessly visionary. Nevertheless it is worth considering whether signs of an approximation to the idea can be traced in international life.

The 20th century began well. There were more

arbitration treaties concluded during the first 10 years than in the whole of the 19th century. The United States declared that as far as they were concerned questions of honour and interest need no longer be excluded from arbitration. Honest efforts were being made to establish an international Court of Justice at the Hague, and Mr Carnegie erected the Palace of Peace to which all nations were to bring their differences, and from which law was to go forth for the world. There were cynics who scoffed, but there were men of goodwill who by the fraternisation of Churches, the promotion of the inter-Parliamentary Union, and numerous conferences and visits, were labouring to promote friendship and trust between the nations. I was one of those who had high hopes in the gradual development of international law and a steady growth in national desire for justice.

Then confidence in the development of a peaceful Europe was shaken by the Italian annexation of Tripoli, and shattered by the German-Austrian note to Serbia which revealed that the will to power, and the will to possess, were the dominant motives of the rulers, and very largely of the people, of Central Europe; that they were still Pagans with whom might and not right was the ruling power. It was a terrible disappointment and a rude awakening to the real forces in the European world. While I believe that our Lord's saying that they that take to the sword shall perish by the sword will be in this case amply verified, yet the ideals of International Law and justice seemed utterly dethroned; and more and more has this been the case, for as the war went on, one after another of the Hague conventions intended to restrain the barbarity of war were ignored.

But nevertheless I am not without hope, and I am encouraged by the following experience. Not very long after the Conciliation Board was established in the mining industry of Durham the men, dissatisfied with the results, gave notice to terminate it. Bishop Westcott, who had been largely instrumental in the creation of the Board, was much distressed. When he expressed his disappointment I replied, " The men are quite right. As a body they do not believe in Conciliation, they are going to try something else. It will not succeed, and then they will return to Conciliation." That is what did actually happen.

It seems to me that it is probable, more than probable, that the horrors and sufferings of this terrible war will have a like result. People in every nation are crying out "never again." But the only way to prevent a recurrence of war is to substitute law and justice for force, and that will send Europe back to the Hague, and to the establishment there of an international court.

There was a striking article recently written by Herr Dernburg, the former German colonial minister, and written for circulation in Germany, in which he said that Germany had been very mistaken in its policy at the Hague in placing spokes in the wheels of suggestions for legal settlement of disputes, and that after the war Germany ought to throw all her influence into strengthening and developing the Hague conferences and courts.

Another significant sign of the times which gives

hope for the future is the treaty with the United States signed on behalf of the United Kingdom on November 14, 1914, *i.e.* three months after the war began, in which both nations bind themselves to refer their disputes to an international commission and not to declare war or begin hostilities until the commission has reported.

Had there been such an agreement between the European powers in August, 1914, there would have been no war. Even if there had been an agreement for a month's delay to enquire into facts there would not have been war.

Is it too much to hope that when this war comes to an end the nations of Europe will protect themselves from the repetition of such disastrous haste as led to this war by mutual agreements based on the American model?

Another sign which may encourage us is the universal desire, nowhere stronger than among the combatants, that a new and better order than the competitive anarchy of the past may be evolved as a result of the war. They desire that competition and greed with all their dire consequences shall cease to be the ruling influences in the relation of states, and men go to death with the hope that out of their death there may spring a better life for Europe. This was touchingly expressed in a letter of a young Austrian soldier which he desired should not be opened till after his death. "We go to battle for justice and freedom and we struggle for a lasting peace....When you read this letter I shall be resting under the sod. My spur to endurance was the thought of the world peace which

is to follow on this world war. I left the world un-
willingly. Do not forget what I lived for, what in the
end I died for: the building up of a better order which
shall create happier men." Yes, this is the universal
desire, and men will not be content in future to permit
statesmen or rulers, foreign ministers or Kaisers, to
enter into secret agreements which may vitally affect
the welfare of the people. Nations have had bitter
experience of the results of secret diplomacy and will
not willingly allow diplomatists or interested financiers
any longer to embroil them with their neighbours
without their knowledge.

Nations as a whole desire fair dealing and to keep
faith. *E.g.* the French nation through their Parliament declared, again and again, their desire and intention of keeping the treaty of Algeciras, and respecting
the independence of Morocco. They were not aware
of the trickery and chicanery by which their agents
were plotting to destroy that independence, and would
have stopped it if they had known.

Nations may be carried away by fits of passion,
but as a rule they desire honest dealing and peace;
and after recent experience they will not tolerate
secret diplomacy in the future to the extent they have
in the past. *E.g.* the entente with France may have
been a wise arrangement, but none of us to this day
knows to what extent it committed us. Even members
of the Cabinet did not know, and it was because they
had been kept in ignorance, and some say purposely
misinformed, that three resigned in August, 1914. It
is monstrous that the nation should be kept in ignorance of that which may imperil the property, the

liberty, the life of every member of the nation. The United States are to be envied for the law which declares that no agreement can be held to bind the U.S. unless it be publicly ratified by the Senate.

Another ground for hope is the consensus of opinion as to the principles which should govern the settlement of peace after the war. If you take those proposals which have been put forth by various societies in England, and those formulated in Holland and other neutral countries, you will find they all agree in demanding:

1.   That justice and not interests ought to be the ruling principle.

2.   That the rights of small nations such as Belgium, Serbia, etc. ought to be respected and they should be free to live their own life.

3.   That an international court be established where differences between nations shall be adjudicated on according to principles of law and justice.

4.   A limitation of armaments.

In other words every one wants the world to be more Christian. But these are not merely Christian utopias, they are largely the ideals Mr Asquith in early stages of the war set before the people as the goal at which they should aim. Here are his words: "The greatest triumph of our time will be the enthronement of the idea of public right as the governing idea of European politics. Room must be found and kept for the independent existence and the free development of the smaller nationalities, each with a corporate consciousness of its own and having exactly as good a title as their more powerful neighbours to a place in the sun.

" There ought to be, perhaps by a slow and gradual process, the substitution for force, for the clash of competing ambition for groupings and alliances the substitution of a real European partnership based on the recognition of equal right and established and enforced by a common will."

And may he never forget his declaration that, " If and when this war is decided in favour of the Allies, it will come at once within the range and before long within the grasp of European statesmanship."

There is much dispute as to how a sanction can be obtained for the decisions of an international court; whether there can be a league of nations which shall maintain a police force to compel any disappointed litigant to accept its provisions, or whether a financial boycott would be better, or whether the power of international opinion will be sufficient. We need not now be much concerned as to the means; if the nations will the end, the means to that end will be found.

There can however be no great and effective reduction of armaments as long as nations live in an atmosphere of mutual suspicion, in fear lest another nation use its superior force to secure its interests. Let cynics say what they will, such goodwill between nations as will enable them to dispense with armaments is not an unattainable ideal. For an illustration of this look across the Atlantic. From the days of the independence of the U.S. till 1814 there were frequent conflicts between the English and the new Republic, the battlefield was round the great lakes, and near Niagara you may see a lofty column commemorating the strife. But in 1814 the representatives of the two powers,

Messrs Bagot and Rice, were men of unusual good sense. They said "What is the use of this rivalry of armaments? If one side builds a battleship the other does the same, then one builds two and so it goes on. Let us agree that neither side shall have more than one ship in each lake, such ship not to exceed 100 tons nor carry more than one 18-lb. gun." That agreement was ratified by the governments of the respective nations, and as a result the forts round the lakes have crumbled to ruin, and for 100 years all along that frontier line extending right across the continent for more than 3000 miles there has been neither fortification nor barrack; and though differences have arisen, acute differences, there has been an underlying conviction that neither the U.S. nor Canada will really attempt to coerce the other, and that the fundamental spirit of goodwill will find a way out of any dispute or conflict of interest. Christian principles are not unpractical, they work whenever they are honestly tried.

The Christian point of view as to international competition is that the only hope of a stable peace lies in Christianising international politics. When the nations learn to act on Christian principles; respect one another, show a spirit of goodwill toward one another; put right above might, and seek justice under forms of law, there will be stable and lasting peace; and it can be secured in no other way. The great need of the time is that Christians shall proclaim their faith. Proclaim with the conviction of the ancient prophets "Thus saith the Lord."

Just as the war broke out a World Alliance for promoting friendly relations among the nations through the Churches was in course of formation. The Alliance, which has over 5000 members in the United Kingdom, has been extending its organisation during the war, and has now in twelve nations groups of men banded together, pledged to bring the influence of the Christian Church to heal as far as possible the wounds of war, mitigate hate, remove misunderstanding, and promote friendship, without which there can be no lasting peace.

In the words of a declaration recently drawn up by the American group of this World Alliance, "We believe it is time for the Christian Church to speak and to act in the strength and assurance of a deep and full loyalty to Jesus Christ. In a time of disillusion and strife when men's hearts faint and doubt let Christian men believe, and try to make all men believe, that the gospel of love by faith and hope is practical, and the only practical way of life for men and nations, and that loyalty to the Kingdom of God is supreme above all other loyalties."

A quotation from an address delivered by President Wilson to the Federal Council of the Churches of Christ in America will serve as a fitting conclusion to this lecture.

"There are a great many arguments about Christianity. The proof of Christianity is written in the biography of the saints—and by the saints I do not mean the technical saints—those whom the Church or the world have picked out and labelled saints—for they are not very numerous—but the people whose lives, whose individual lives have been transformed by Christianity. It is the only force in the world that I have ever heard of that does actually transform life. And the proof of that transformation is to be found all over the Christian world....Men begin suddenly to erect great spiritual standards over the little spiritual standards which they have heretofore professed, and will walk smiling to the stake in order that their soul may be true to themselves. There is not anything else that does that. There is something that is analogous to it and that is patriotism. Men will go into the fire of battle and freely give their lives for something greater than themselves—their duty to their country, and there is a pretty fine analogy between patriotism and Christianity. It is the devotion of the spirit to something greater and nobler than itself.

"These are the transforming influences. All the transforming influences of the world are unselfish. There is not a single selfish force in the world that is not touched with sinister power, and the Church is the only embodiment of the things which are entirely unselfish, the principles of self-sacrifice and devotion. Surely this is the instrumentality by which communities may be transformed and led to things that are great: and surely there is nothing in which the Church ought not to be the leader, and in which it ought not to be the vital actual centre."

For EU product safety concerns, contact us at Calle de José Abascal, 56–1°, 28003 Madrid, Spain or eugpsr@cambridge.org.

www.ingramcontent.com/pod-product-compliance
Ingram Content Group UK Ltd.
Pitfield, Milton Keynes, MK11 3LW, UK
UKHW012328130625
459647UK00009B/133